SHAKESPEARE

HAMLET

NOTES

COLES EDITORIAL BOARD

CONTENTS

Characters

Structure

Meaning

Style

WILLIAM SHAKESPEARE
LIFE AND WORKS
Biographical Sketch

With the epithet "Dear Son of Memory", Milton praised Shakespeare as one constantly in our memories and brother of the Muses. Certainly no other author has held such sway over the literary world, undiminished through some three and a half centuries of shifting artistic tastes. Shakespeare's plots and his characters have continued to be a living reality for us; as his well known contemporary Ben Jonson wrote, in a familiar tribute, "Thou . . . art alive still, while thy Booke doth live,/ And we have wits to read, and praise to give."

The Early Years

Despite such acclaim and the scholarship it has spawned, our knowledge of Shakespeare's life is sketchy, filled with more questions than answers, even after we prune away the misinformation accumulated over the years. He was baptized on April 26, 1564, in Holy Trinity Church, Stratford-on-Avon. As it was customary to baptize children a few days after birth, we conjecture that he was born on April 23. The monument erected in Stratford states that he died on April 23, 1616, in his fifty-third year.

William was the third child of John Shakespeare, who came to Stratford from Snitterfield before 1532 as a "whyttawer" (tanner) and glover, and Mary Arden, daughter of a wealthy "gentleman of worship" from Wilmecote. They married around 1557. Since John Shakespeare owned one house on Greenhill Street and two on Henley Street, we cannot be certain where William was born, though the Henley Street shrine draws many tourists each year. William's two older sisters died in infancy, but three brothers and two other sisters survived at least into childhood.

Shakespeare's father was fairly well-to-do, dealing in farm products and wool, and owning considerable property in Stratford. After holding a series of minor municipal offices he was elected alderman in 1565, high bailiff (roughly similar to the mayor of today) in 1568, and chief alderman in 1571. There are no records of young Will Shakespeare's education (though there are many unfounded legends), but he undoubtedly attended the town school maintained by the burgesses, which prepared its students for the universities. Ben Jonson's line about Shakespeare's having "small *Latine*, and lesse *Greeke*" refers not to his education but to his lack of indebtedness to the classical writers and dramatists.

On November 27, 1582, a licence to marry was issued to "Willelmum Shaxpere *et* Annam Whateley *de* Temple Grafton," and on

1

the next day a marriage bond for "Willm Shagspere" and "Anne Hathwey of Stratford" was signed by Fulk Sandells and John Richardson, farmers of Stratford. This bond stated that there was no "lawful let or impediment by reason of any precontract, consanguinity, affinity, or by any other lawful means whatsoever"; thus "William and Anne (were) to be married together with once asking of the banns of matrimony." The problem of Anne Whateley has led many researchers and some detractors to argue all kinds of improbabilities, such as the existence of two different Shakespeares and the forging of documents to conceal Shakespeare's true identity. The actual explanation seems to be simple: the clerk who made the marriage licence entry apparently copied the name "Whateley" from a preceding entry, as a glance at the full sheet suggests. (Incidentally, Nicholas Rowe in his life of Shakespeare, published in 1709, well before the discovery of these marriage records, gave Anne's name as Hathaway.) The problems of marriage with Anne Hathaway — he was eighteen and she was twenty-six — and of the bond have caused similar consternation. Why did these two marry when there was such a discrepancy of age? Why only one saying of the banns (rather than the usual three)? Why the emphasis on a possible legal impediment? The answer here is not simple or definite, but the birth of a daughter Susanna, baptized at Holy Trinity on May 26, 1583, seems to explain the odd circumstances. It should be recognized, however, that an engagement to marry was considered legally binding in those days (we still have breach-of-promise suits today) and that premarital relations were not unusual or frowned upon when an engagement had taken place. The circumstances already mentioned, Shakespeare's ensuing activities, and his will bequeathing to Anne "my second best bed with the furniture" have suggested to some that their marriage was not entirely happy. Their other children, the twins Hamnet and Judith, were christened on February 2, 1585.

Theatrical Life

Shakespeare's years before and immediately after the time of his marriage are not charted, but rumor has him as an apprentice to a master butcher or as a country teacher or an actor with some provincial company. He is supposed to have run away from whatever he was doing for livelihood and to have gone to London, where he soon attached himself to some theatrical group. At this time there were only two professional houses established in the London environs, The Theatre (opened in 1576) and The Curtain (opened in 1577). His first connection with the theater was reputedly as holder of horses; that is, one of the stage crew, but a most inferior assignment. Thereafter he became an actor (perhaps at this time he met Ben Jonson), a writer, and a director. Such experience had its mark in the theatricality of his plays. We do know that he was established in London by 1592, when Robert Greene

2

lamented in *A Groatsworth of Wit* (September, 1592) that professional actors had gained priority in the theater over university-trained writers like himself: "There is an upstart Crow, beautified with our feathers, that with his *Tygers hart wrapt in a Players hyde*, supposes he is as well able to bombast out a lanke verse as the best of you: and beeing an absolute *Iohannes fac totum* (Jack-of-all-trades), is in his owne conceit the onely Shake-scene in a countrey." An apology for Greene's ill-humored statement by Henry Chettle, the editor of the pamphlet, appeared around December 1592 in *Kind-Hart's Dream*.

Family Affairs

To return to the known details of family life, Shakespeare's son Hamnet was buried at Stratford on August 11, 1596; his father was given a coat of arms on October 20, 1596; and he purchased New Place (a refurbished tourist attraction today) on May 4, 1597. The London playwright obviously had not severed connections with his birthplace, and he was reflecting his new affluence by being known as William Shakespeare of Stratford-upon-Avon, in the County of Warwick, Gentleman. His father was buried in Stratford on September 8, 1601; his mother, on September 9, 1608. His daughter Susanna married Dr. John Hall on June 5, 1607, and they had a child named Elizabeth. His other daughter, Judith, married Thomas Quiney on February 10, 1616, without special licence, during Lent and was thus excommunicated. Shakespeare revised his will on March 25, 1616, and was buried on April 25, 1616 (according to the parish register). A monument by Gerard Janssen was erected in the Holy Trinity chancel in 1623 but many, like Milton several years later, protested:

> What needs my *Shakespeare* for his honour'd Bones,
> The labour of an age in piled Stone, . . .
> Thou in our wonder and astonishment
> Hast built thy self a live-long Monument.

Shakespeare's Writings

Order of Appearance

Dating of Shakespeare's early plays, while based on inconclusive evidence, has tended to hover around the early 1590's. Almost certainly it is his chronicles of Henry the Sixth that Philip Henslowe, an important theatrical manager of the day, referred to in his diary as being performed during March-May, 1592. An allusion to these plays also occurs in Thomas Nashe's *Piers Penniless His Supplication to the Devil* (August, 1592). Greene's quotation about a tiger is a paraphrase of "O tiger's heart wrapt in a woman's hide" from *Henry VI*, Part III.

The first published work to come from Shakespeare's hand was *Venus and Adonis* (1593), a long stanzaic poem, dedicated to Henry

Wriothesley, Earl of Southampton. A year later *The Rape of Lucrece* appeared, also dedicated to Southampton. Perhaps poetry was pursued during these years because the London theaters were closed as a result of a virulent siege of plague. The *Sonnets*, published in 1609, may owe something to Southampton, who had become Shakespeare's patron. Perhaps some were written as early as the first few years of the 1590's. They were mentioned (along with a number of plays) in 1598 by Francis Meres in his *Palladis Tamia*, and sonnets 138 and 144 were printed without authority by William Jaggard in *The Passionate Pilgrim* (1599).

There is a record of a performance of *A Comedy of Errors* at Gray's Inn (one of the law colleges) on December 28, 1594, and, during early 1595, Shakespeare was paid, along with the famous actors Richard Burbage and William Kempe, for performances before the Queen by the Lord Chamberlain's Men, a theatrical company formed the year before. The company founded the Globe Theatre on the south side of the Thames in 1599 and became the King's Men when James ascended the throne. Records show frequent payments to the company through its general manager John Heminge. From 1595 through 1614 there are numerous references to real estate transactions and other legal matters, to many performances, and to various publications connected with Shakespeare.

Order of Publication

The first plays to be printed were *Titus Andronicus* around February, 1594, and the garbled versions of *Henry VI*, Parts II and III in 1594. (Some scholars, however, question whether the last two are versions of *Henry VI*, Parts II and III, and some dispute Shakespeare's authorship.) Thereafter *Richard III* appeared in 1597 and 1598; *Richard II*, in 1597 and twice in 1598; *Romeo and Juliet*, in 1597 (a pirated edition) and 1599, and many others. Some of the plays appear in individual editions, with or without Shakespeare's name on the title page,but eighteen are known only from their appearance in the first collected volume (the so-called First Folio) of 1623. The editors were Heminge and Henry Condell, another member of Shakespeare's company. *Pericles* was omitted from the First Folio although it had appeared in 1609, 1611, and 1619; it was added to the Third Folio in 1664.

There was reluctance to publish plays at this time for various reasons; many plays were carelessly written for fast production; collaboration was frequent; plays were not really considered *reading* matter; they were sometimes circulated in manuscript; and the theatrical company, not the author, owned the rights. Those plays given individual publication appeared in a quarto, so named from the size of the page. A single sheet of paper was folded twice to make four leaves (thus *quarto*) or eight pages; these four leaves constitute one signature (one section of a bound book). A page measures about 6¾ in. x 8½ in. On the other hand, a folio sheet is folded once to make two leaves or four pages; three sheets, or twelve pages, constitute a signature. The page is approximately 8½ in. x 13⅜ in.

Authorized publication occurred when a company disbanded, when money was needed but rights were to be retained, when a play failed or ran into licensing difficulties (thus, hopefully, the printed work would justify the play against the criticism), or when a play had been pirated. Authorized editions are called good quartos. Piratical publication might occur when the manuscript of a play had circulated privately, when a member of a company desired money for himself, or when a stenographer or memorizer took the play down in the theater (such a version was recognizable by inclusion of stage directions derived from an eyewitness, by garbled sections, etc.). Pirated editions are called bad quartos; there are at least five bad quartos of Shakespeare's plays.

Authenticity of Works

Usually thirty-seven plays are printed in modern collections of Shakespeare's works but some recent scholars have urged the addition of two more: *Edward III* and *Two Noble Kinsmen*. A case has also been advanced, unconvincingly, for a fragment of the play on Sir Thomas More. At times, six of the generally-accepted plays have been questioned: *Henry VI*, Parts I, II and III, *Timon of Athens*, *Pericles* and *Henry VIII*. The first four are usually accepted today (one hopes all question concerning *Timon* has finally ended), but if Shakespeare did not write these plays in their entirety, he certainly wrote parts of them. Of course, collaboration in those days was commonplace. Aside from the two long narrative poems already mentioned and the sonnets (Nos. 1-152, but not Nos. 153-154), Shakespeare's poetic output is uncertain. *The Passionate Pilgrim* (1599) contains only five authenticated poems (two sonnets and three verses from *Love's Labour's Lost*); *The Phoenix and the Turtle* (1601) may be his, but the authenticity of *A Lover's Complaint* (appended to the sonnets) is highly questionable.

Who Was Shakespeare?

At this point we might mention a problem that has plagued Shakespeare study for over a century: who was Shakespeare? Those who would like to make the author of the plays someone else — Francis Bacon or the Earl of Oxford or even Christopher Marlowe (dead long before most of the plays were written) — have used the lack of information of Shakespeare's early years and the confusion in the evidence we have been examining to advance their candidate. But the major arguments against Shakespeare show the source of these speculators' disbelief to be in classconscious snobbery and perhaps in a perverse adherence to minority opinion. The most common argument is that no one of Shakespeare's background, lack of education, and lack of aristocratic experience could know all that the author knew. But study will reveal that such information was readily available in various popular

5

sources, that some of it lies in the literary sources used for the play, and that Shakespeare was probably not totally lacking in education or in social decorum. The more significant question of style and tone is not dealt with — nor could it successfully be raised. Bacon, for example, no matter how much we admire his mind and his writings, exhibits a writing style diametrically opposite to Shakespeare's, a style most unpoetic and often flat. The student would be wise not to waste time rehashing these unfounded theories. No such question was raised in the seventeenth or eighteenth centuries, and no serious student of the plays today doubts that Shakespeare *was* Shakespeare.

Shakespeare's Plays

Exact dates for Shakespeare's plays remain a source of debate among scholars. The following serve only as a general frame of reference.

	COMEDIES	TRAGEDIES	HISTORIES
1591			Henry VI, Part I
1592	Comedy of Errors		Henry VI, Part II
1592	Two Gentlemen of Verona		Henry VI, Part III
1593	Love's Labour's Lost	Titus Andronicus	Richard III
1594			King John
1595	Midsummer Night's Dream	Romeo and Juliet	Richard II
1596	Merchant of Venice		
1596	Taming of the Shrew		
1597			Henry IV, Part I
1598	Much Ado About Nothing		Henry IV, Part II
1599	As You Like It	Julius Caesar	
1599	Merry Wives of Windsor		Henry V
1601	Twelfth Night	Hamlet	
1602	Troilus and Cressida		
1602	All's Well That Ends Well		
1604	Measure for Measure	Othello	
1605		King Lear	
1606		Macbeth	
1607		Timon of Athens	
1607		Antony and Cleopatra	
1608	Pericles		
1609		Coriolanus	
1610	Cymbeline		
1611	Winter's Tale		
1611	Tempest		
1613			Henry VIII

Shakespeare's England

The world of Elizabethan and Jacobean England was a world of growth and change. The great increase in the middle class, and in the population as a whole, demanded a new economy and means of livelihood, a new instrument of government (one recognizing "rights" and changed class structure), a new social code and a broad base of entertainment. The invention of printing a century before had contributed to that broader base, but it was the theater that supplied the more immediate needs of the greatest numbers. The theater grew and along with it came less-educated, more money-conscious writers, who gave the people what they wanted: entertainment. But Shakespeare, having passed through a brief period of hack writing, proceeded to set down important ideas in memorable language throughout most of his career. His plays, particularly the later ones, have been analyzed by recent critics in terms of literary quality through their metaphor, verse-line, relationships with psychology and myth, and elaborate structure. Yet Shakespeare was a man of the stage, and the plays were written to be performed. Only this will fully account for the humor of a deadly serious play like *Hamlet* or the spectacle of a *Coriolanus*.

Life in London

During Shakespeare's early years there, London was a walled city of about 200,000, with seven gates providing access to the city from the east, north, and west. It was geographically small and crisscrossed by narrow little streets and lanes. The various wards each had a parish church that dominated the life of the close-knit community. To the south and outside were slums and the haunts of criminal types, and farther out were the agricultural lands and huge estates. As the population increased and the central area declined, the fashionable people of the city moved toward the west, where the palace of Westminster lay. Houses were generally rented out floor by floor and sometimes room by room. Slums were common within the city, too, though close to pleasant enough streets and squares. "Merrie Olde England" was not really clean, nor were its people, for in those days there were no sewers or drains except the gutter in the middle of the street, into which garbage would be emptied to be floated off by the rain to Fleet ditch or Moor ditch. Plague was particularly ravaging in 1592, 1593-94 (when the theaters were closed to avoid contamination) and 1603. Medical knowledge, of course, was slight; ills were "cured" by amputation, leeching, blood-letting and cathartics. The city was (and still is) dominated by St. Paul's Cathedral, around which booksellers clustered on Paternoster Row.

Religious Atmosphere

Of great significance for the times was religion. Under Elizabeth, a state church had developed; it was Protestant in nature and was called Anglican (or today, Episcopalian) but it had arisen from Henry VIII's break with the Pope and from a compromise with the Roman Catholics who had gained power under Mary Tudor.

The Church of England was headed by the Archbishop of Canter bury, who was to be an increasingly important figure in the early part of the seventeenth century. There were also many schismatic groups, which generally desired further departures from Roman Catholicism. Calvinists were perhaps the most numerous and important of the Protestant groups. The Puritans, who were Calvinist, desired to "purify" the church of ritual and certain dogmas, but during the 1590's they were lampooned as extremists in dress and conduct.

Political Milieu

During Shakespeare's lifetime there were two monarchs: Elizabeth, 1558-1603, and James I, 1603-1625. Elizabeth was the daughter of Henry VIII and Anne Boleyn, his second wife, who was executed in 1536. After Henry's death, his son by his third wife, Jane Seymore (executed in 1537), reigned as Edward VI. He was followed by Mary Tudor, daughter of Henry's first wife, Catherine of Aragon. Mary was a Roman Catholic, who tried to put down religious dissension by persecution of both Protestants and Catholics. Nor did her marriage to Philip II of Spain endear her to the people.

Elizabeth's reign was troubled by many offers of marriage, particularly from Spanish and French nobles — all Roman Catholic — and by the people's concern for an heir to the throne. English suitors generally cancelled one another out by intrigue or aggressiveness. One of the most prominent was the Earl of Essex, Robert Devereux, who fell in and out of favor; he apparently attempted to take over the reins of control, only to be captured, imprisoned and executed in February, 1601. One claimant to the throne was Mary of Scotland, a Roman Catholic and widow of Francis II of France. She was the second cousin of Elizabeth, tracing her claim through her grandmother, who was Henry VIII's sister. Finally, settlement came with Elizabeth's acceptance of Mary's son as heir apparent, though Mary was to be captured, tried and executed for treason in 1587. Mary had abdicated the throne of Scotland in 1567 in favor of her son, James VI. His ascent to the throne of England in 1603 as James I joined the two kingdoms for the first time, although Scotland during the seventeenth century often acted independently of England.

Contemporary Events

Political and religious problems were intermingled in the celebrated Gunpowder Plot. Angry over fines that were levied upon those not attending Church of England services — primarily Roman Catholics — and offended by difficulties over papal envoys, a group of Catholics plotted to blow up Parliament, and James with it, at its first session on November 5, 1605. A cache of gunpowder was stored in the cellar, guarded by various conspirators, among them Guy Fawkes. The plot was discovered before it could be carried out and Fawkes, on duty at the time, was apprehended. The execution of the plotters and the triumph of the anti-Papists led in succeeding years to celebrations in the streets and the hanging of Fawkes in effigy.

Among the most noteworthy public events during these times were the wars with the Spanish, which included the defeat of the Spanish Armada in 1588, the battle in the Lowlands in 1590-1594, the expedition to Cadiz under Essex in 1596 and the expedition to the Azores (the Islands Expedition), also under Essex, in 1597. With trading companies especially set up for colonization and exploitation, travel excited the imagination of the people: here was a new way of life, here were new customs brought back by the sailors and merchants, here was a new dream world to explore.

In all, the years from around 1590 to 1601 were trying ones for English people, relieved only by the news from abroad, the new affluence and the hope for the future under James. Writers of the period frequently reflect, however, the disillusionment and sadness of those difficult times.

The Elizabethan Theater

Appearance

The Elizabethan playhouse developed from the medieval inn with its rooms grouped around a courtyard into which a stage was built. This pattern was used in The Theatre, built by James Burbage in 1576: a square frame building (later round or octagonal) with a square yard, three tiers of galleries, each jutting out over the one below, and a stage extending into the middle of the yard, where people stood or sat on improvised seats. There was no cover over the yard or stage and lighting was therefore natural. Thus performances were what we might consider late matinees or early evening performances; in summer, daylight continues in London until around ten o'clock.

Other theaters were constructed during the ensuing years: The Curtain in 1577, The Rose in 1587 (on Bankside), The Swan in 1595 (also Bankside) and Shakespeare's playhouse, The Globe, in 1599 (not far from The Rose). There is still some question about the exact dimensions of this house, but it seems to have been octagonal, each side measuring about 36 feet, with an over-all diameter of 84 feet. It was about 33 feet to the eaves, and the yard was 56 feet in diameter. Three sides were used for backstage and to serve the needs of the players. There was no curtain or proscenium, hence the spectators became part of the action. Obviously, the actors' asides and soliloquies were effective under these conditions.

There was no real scenery and there were only a few major props; thus the lines of the play had to reveal locations and movement, changes in time or place, etc. In this way, too, it was easier to establish a nonrealistic setting, for all settings were created in words. On either side of the stage were doors, within the flooring were trapdoors (for entrances of ghosts, etc.), and behind the main stage was the inner stage or recess. Here, indoor scenes (such as a court or a bedchamber) were played, and some props could be used because the inner stage was usually concealed by a curtain when not in use. It might also have served to hide someone behind the ever-present arras, like Polonius in *Hamlet*. The "chamber" was on the second level, with windows and a balcony. On the third level was another chamber, primarily for musicians.

Actors

An acting company such as the Lord Chamberlain's Men was a fellowship of ten to fifteen sharers with some ten to twelve extras, three or four boys (often to play women's roles) who might become full sharers, and stagehands. There were rival companies, each with its leading dramatist and leading tragic actor and clown. The Lord Admiral's Men, organized in 1594, boasted Ben Jonson and the tragedian Edward Alleyn. Some of the rivalry of this War of the Theaters is reflected in the speeches of Hamlet, who also comments on the ascendancy and unwarranted popularity of the children's companies (like the Children of Blackfriars) in the late 1590's.

The company dramatist, of course, had to think in terms of the members of his company as he wrote his play. He had to make use of the physical features and peculiar talents of the actors, making sure, besides, that there was a role for each member. The fact that women's parts were taken by boys imposed obvious limitations on the range of action. Accordingly, we often find women characters impersonating men; for example, Robert Goffe played Portia in *The Merchant of Venice*, and Portia impersonates a male lawyer in the important trial scene. Goffe also played Juliet, and Anne in *Richard III*, and Oberon in *Midsummer Night's Dream*. The influence of an actor on the playwright can be seen, on the one hand, by noting the "humor" characters portrayed so competently by Thomas Pope, who was a choleric Mercutio in *Romeo*, a melancholic Jaques in *As You Like It*, and a sanguinary Falstaff in *Henry IV*, Part I; and by comparing, on the other hand, the clown Bottom in *Midsummer Night's Dream*, played in a frolicsome manner by William Kempe, with the clown Feste in *Twelfth Night*, sung and danced by Robert Armin. Obviously, too, if a certain kind of character was not available within the company, then that kind of character could not be written into the play. The approach was decidedly different from ours today, where the play almost always comes first and the casting of roles second. The plays were performed in a repertory system, with a different play each afternoon. The average life of a play was about ten performances.

History of the Drama

English drama goes back to native forms developed from playlets presented at Church holidays. Mystery plays dealt with biblical stories

10

such as the Nativity or the Passion, and miracle plays usually depicted the lives of saints. The merchant and craft guilds that came to own and produce the cycles of plays were the forerunners of the theatrical companies of Shakespeare's time. The kind of production these cycles received, either as moving pageants in the streets or as staged shows in a churchyard, influenced the late sixteenth-century production of a secular play: there was an intimacy with the audience and there was a great reliance on words rather than setting and props. Similar involvement with the stage action is experienced by audiences of the arena theater of today.

The morality play, the next form to develop, was an allegory of the spiritual conflict between good and evil in the soul of man. The *dramatis personae* were abstract virtues and vices, with at least one man representing Mankind (or Everyman, as the most popular of these plays was titled). Some modern critics see *Othello* as a kind of morality play in which the soul of Othello is vied for by the aggressively evil Iago (as a kind of Satanic figure) and passively good Desdemona (as a personification of Christian faith in all men). The Tudor interlude — a short, witty, visual play — may have influenced the subplot of the Elizabethan play with its low-life and jesting and visual tricks. In mid-sixteenth century appeared the earliest known English comedies, Nicholas Udall's *Ralph Roister Doister* and *Gammer Gurton's Needle* (of uncertain authorship). Both show the influence of the Roman comic playwright Plautus. Shakespeare's *Comedy of Errors*, performed in the 1590's, was an adaptation of Plautus' *Menaechmi*, both plays featuring twins and an involved story of confused identities. The influence of the Roman tragedian Seneca can be traced from Thomas Norton and Thomas Sackville in *Gorboduc* to *Hamlet*. Senecan tragedy is a tragedy of revenge, characterized by many deaths, much blood-letting, ghosts, feigned madness and the motif of a death for a death.

Shakespeare's Artistry

Plots

Generally, a Shakespearean play has two plots: a main plot and a subplot. The subplot reflects the main plot and is often concerned with inferior characters. Two contrasting examples will suffice: Lear and his daughters furnish the characters for the main plot of filial love and ingratitude, whereas Gloucester and his sons enact the same theme in the subplot; Lear and Gloucester both learn that outward signs of love may be false. In *Midsummer Night's Dream*, the town workmen (Quince, Bottom *et al*.) put on a tragic play in such a hilarious way that it turns the subject of the play — love so strong that the hero will kill himself if his loved one dies first — into farce, but this in the main plot is the "serious" plight of the four mixed-up lovers. In both examples Shakespeare has reinforced his points by subplots dealing with the same subject as the main plot.

Sources

The plots of the Elizabethan plays were usually adapted from other sources. "Originality" was not the sought quality; a kind of variation on a theme was. It was felt that one could better evaluate the playwright's worth by seeing what he did with a familiar tale. What he stressed, how he stressed it, how he restructured the familiar elements — these were the important matters. Shakespeare closely followed Sir Thomas North's very popular translation of Plutarch's *Life of Marcus Antonius*, for example, in writing *Antony and Cleopatra*; and he modified Robert Greene's *Pandosto* and combined it with the Pygmalion myth in *The Winter's Tale*, while drawing the character of Autolycus from certain pamphlets written by Greene. The only plays for which sources have not been clearly determined are *Love's Labour's Lost* (probably based on contemporary events) and *The Tempest* (possibly based on some shipwreck account from travellers to the New World).

Verse and Prose

There is a mixture of verse and prose in the plays, partially because plays fully in verse were out of fashion. Greater variety could thus be achieved and character or atmosphere could be more precisely delineated. Elevated passages, philosophically significant ideas, speeches by men of high rank are in verse, but comic and light parts, speeches including dialect or broken English, and scenes that move more rapidly or simply give mundane information are in prose. The poetry is almost always blank verse (iambic pentameter lines without rhyme). Rhyme is used, however (particularly the couplet), to mark the close of scenes or an important action. Rhyme also serves as a cue for the entrance of another actor or some off-stage business, to point to a change of mood or thought, as a forceful opening after a passage of prose, to convey excitement or passion or sentimentality and to distinguish characters.

Shakespeare's plays may be divided into three general categories, though some plays are not readily classified and further subdivisions may be suggested within a category.

The History Play

The history play, or chronicle, may tend to tragedy, like *Richard II*, or to comedy, like *Henry IV*, Part I. It is a chronicle of some royal personage, often altered for dramatic purposes, even to the point of falsification of the facts. Its popularity may have resulted from the rising of nationalism of the English, nurtured by their successes against the Spanish, their developing trade and colonization, and their rising prestige as a world power. The chronicle was considered a political guide, like the popular *Mirror for Magistrates*, a collection of writings showing what happens when an important leader falls through some error in his ways, his thinking or his personality. Thus the history play counseled the right path by negative, if not positive, means. Accordingly, it is difficult to call *Richard II* a tragedy, since Richard was wrong and his wrongness harmed his people. The political philosophy of Shakespeare's day seemed to favor the view that all usurpation was bad and should be corrected, but not by further usurpation. When that original usurpation had been established, through an heir's ascension to the throne, it was to be accepted. Then any rebellion against the "true" king would be a rebellion against God.

Tragedy

Tragedy in simple terms meant that the protagonist died. Certain concepts drawn from Aristotle's *Poetics* require a tragic hero of high standing, who must oppose some conflicting force, either external or internal. The tragic hero should be dominated by a *hamartia* (a so-called tragic flaw, but really an *excess* of some character trait, e.g., pride, or *hubris*), and it is this *hamartia* that leads to his downfall and, because of his status, to the downfall of others. The action presented in the tragedy must be recognizable to the audience as real and potential: through seeing it enacted, the audience has its passion (primarily suffering) raised, and the conclusion of the action thus brings release from that passion (*catharsis*). A more meaningful way of looking at tragedy in the Elizabethan theater, however, is to see it as that which occurs when essential good (like Hamlet) is wasted (through disaster or death) in the process of driving out evil (such as Claudius represents).

Comedy

Comedy in simple terms meant that the play ended happily for the protagonists. Sometimes the comedy depends on exaggerations of man's eccentricities — comedy of humors; sometimes the comedy is romantic and far-fetched. The romantic comedy was usually based on a mix-up in events or confused identity of characters, particularly by disguise. It moved toward tragedy in that an important person might die and the mix-up might never be unraveled; but in the nick of time something happens or someone appears (sometimes illogically or unexpectedly) and saves the day. It reflects the structure of myth by moving from happiness to despair to resurrection. *The Winter's Tale* is a perfect example of this, for the happiness of the first part is banished with Hermione's exile and Perdita's abandonment; tragedy is near when the lost baby, Perdita, cannot be found and Hermione is presumed dead, but Perdita reappears, as does Hermione, a statue that suddenly comes to life. Lost identities are established and confusions disappear but the mythic-comic nature of the play is seen in the reuniting of the mother, Hermione, a kind of Ceres, with her daughter, Perdita, a kind of Prosperina. Spring returns, summer will bring the harvest, and the winter of the tale is left behind — for a little while.

What is it, then, that makes Shakespeare's art so great? Perhaps we see in it a whole spectrum of humanity, treated impersonally, but with kindness and understanding. We seldom meet in Shakespeare a weeping philosopher: he may criticize, but he criticizes both sides. After he has done so, he gives the impression of saying, Well, that's the way life is; people will always be like that — don't get upset about it. This is probably the key to the Duke's behavior in *Measure for Measure* — a most unbitter comedy despite former labels. Only in *Hamlet* does Shakespeare not seem to fit this statement; it is the one play that Shakespeare, the person, enters.

As we grow older and our range of experience widens, so, too, does Shakespeare's range seem to expand. Perhaps this lies in the ambiguities of his own materials, which allow for numerous individual readings. We meet our own experiences — and they are ours alone, we think — expressed in phrases that we thought our own or of our own discovery. What makes Shakespeare's art so great, then, is his ability to say so much to so many people in such memorable language: he is himself "the show and gaze o' the time."

HAMLET
Plot Summary

A ghost, which looks like the late king of Denmark, has appeared to sentries at the Castle of Elsinore, which is armed in case of attack from Fortinbras, prince of Norway. The sentries have brought Horatio, a friend of Hamlet's, to observe the ghost; it appears, disappears, reappears, and leaves a final time as the cock crows. Later in the day the king of Denmark, Claudius, brother to the late king who had defeated Fortinbras' father, sends messengers to the king of Norway (Fortinbras' uncle), gives Laertes (Polonius' son) permission to return to France, and inquires about Hamlet's melancholic state. Hamlet's father, we learn, has been dead only two months, but his mother has married his uncle, who has now become king. Horatio informs Hamlet of the ghost; they arrange to meet that night to see whether it will appear.

At Polonius' house, Laertes advises his sister Ophelia not to trust Hamlet or be seduced by him. Then Polonius, an adviser to the king, says goodbye to Laertes, advising him to remain aloof from entanglements with his fellow man. Next he cautions Ophelia not to believe Hamlet and to report to him her contacts with the prince. That night the ghost appears again, beckoning Hamlet to a private talk. The ghost states that it is the spirit of Hamlet's father, who has been murdered by the present king. While he slept in his orchard, his brother Claudius poured poison in his ear. Hamlet is told to set things right, but to leave his mother's punishment to heaven.

Polonius sends Reynaldo to spy on Laertes in France and then questions Ophelia about an encounter with Hamlet. Polonius concludes that Hamlet's thwarted love has made him mad. The king commissions Rosencrantz and Guildenstern, friends of Hamlet, to find out what is troubling him. Fortinbras' successes are recounted, and Polonius advances his theory about Hamlet's disposition, giving as evidence a letter written to Ophelia. Hamlet enters and Polonius tries to get him to explain what is bothering him. Rosencrantz and Guildenstern next interview Hamlet, who is aware of their true purpose. The conversation turns to a traveling troupe of actors who have come to provide entertainment for the royal assemblage. After talk of plays and players, an actor recites lines about the death of Priam, king of Troy. Hamlet arranges for the actor to insert a playlet into the evening performance. He then regrets his inability to act upon his plan of revenge.

Further preparations are made to spy on Hamlet. The king, Polonius, and Ophelia conceal themselves while Hamlet meditates on what course of action he should take. Suspicious of Ophelia, who is instructed to enter into a conversation with him, Hamlet dismisses her to a nunnery. The king recognizes what is troubling Hamlet and therefore decides to send Hamlet to England. Soon the play is presented. Horatio is to observe the king's reaction to it, and Hamlet sits at Ophelia's feet. There is a pantomime, followed by a play, both of which show a king being murdered as the ghost had declared Hamlet's father was. The king rises and rushes away. Rosencrantz and Guildenstern, and then Polonius, inform Hamlet that his mother wishes to speak to him in her sitting room. Again Polonius will spy and the queen is to try to get at the reason behind Hamlet's behavior. On his way there, Hamlet sees the king at prayer, but delays killing him, so that he won't be saved because of being in a state of grace. Hamlet does not hear the king state his lack of real repentance. Polonius has preceded Hamlet to the queen's room and hidden himself behind a tapestry. The queen scolds Hamlet for offending the king. He speaks roughly to her, she cries for help, Polonius joins her calls, and Hamlet, thinking he is the king, kills him with his sword. Again Hamlet reproaches his mother for her complicity in the murder. He speaks with the ghost, which is unseen and unheard by the queen. He accuses his mother further, and reveals that he knows of the plan to send him to England to get rid of him.

The queen tells the king about her interview with Hamlet and his slaying of Polonius. Rosencrantz and Guildenstern are sent to find the body, but Hamlet, who knows its whereabouts, speaks in riddles to them and then to the king. Hamlet is informed officially that he is being sent to England, and we learn that he is to be killed there. In the next scene, Fortinbras passes through Denmark to win back a little patch of ground belonging to Poland. Hamlet, observing this exposure to death and danger "even for an eggshell," is strengthened into bloody resolution to avenge his father. Ophelia has gone mad and sings incoherently of love and death. The people are riotous because of Polonius' death and shout that Laertes shall be king. Laertes then enters, set on revenge; the king tries to calm, but not dissuade him. The sight of Ophelia adds to Laertes' grief. Meanwhile, we learn from a letter delivered to Horatio that Hamlet has escaped with the help of pirates who boarded the ship. The king has apparently explained to Laertes how his father came to be killed, and receiving Hamlet's letter stating that he has returned to Denmark alone, the king plots the death of Hamlet in a duel with Laertes. Laertes has previously acquired poison in which he will dip his sword to insure Hamlet's death. The king is to prepare a poisoned drink, which he will offer to Hamlet during the duel. The act ends with the queen's report of Ophelia's death by drowning.

The final act begins with the sardonic humor of two gravediggers preparing a grave for Ophelia. Hamlet and Horatio observe them and remark on the remains of the dead that are unearthed. A funeral procession enters. Laertes protests that more rites should be said, but the priest refuses because Ophelia's death was "doubtful." Laertes, unable to control his grief, leaps into the grave, and Hamlet, finally aware of who has died, also leaps in. Each protests stronger feelings of grief, and they fight until attendants part them. A little later, Hamlet relates what occurred during his trip to England. He discovered the plot to kill him and altered the orders so that Rosencrantz and Guildenstern would be killed. Osric appears to bring a challenge for Hamlet from Laertes. The duel follows, the foils and the wine having been prepared. Hamlet is urged to drink, but does not. The queen unwittingly drinks the wine, Laertes wounds Hamlet, the swords are exchanged in a scuffle, and Hamlet wounds Laertes. The queen dies. Laertes falls and denounces the king, who is stabbed by Hamlet. Both the king and Laertes die. Hamlet tells Horatio to tell his story, recommending that Fortinbras be elected king, and then dies. Fortinbras enters with English ambassadors, who inform the assemblage that Rosencrantz and Guildenstern are dead. Fortinbras has Hamlet nobly carried from the scene.

Sources of the Play

Sound commentary on this tragedy also calls for a knowledge of the sources available to Shakespeare when he decided to dramatize the story of Hamlet, prince of Denmark. Time and again, critics have turned to an earlier version or versions in their efforts to find answers to questions which inevitably arise. Moreover, knowledge of earlier versions makes possible a surer appreciation of Shakespeare's accomplishment.

The story of Hamlet goes far back in Scandinavian legend, in this respect bearing comparison with the Anglo-Saxon account of Beowulf. The earliest surviving literary tale of Hamlet is found in Saxo Grammaticus' *Historia Danica* (c 1200). For his *Histoires Tragiques* (1756), a widely popular collection of tales in French, François de Belleforest adopted it, with basic themes, prototypes of characters, and story elements later to be found in Shakespeare's play. These elements include adultery, fratricide, revenge, assumed madness, and the villain's use of spies. Nevertheless, the differences between Belleforest's version and Shakespeare's are great and significant.

If this were the only version of the Hamlet story available to Shakespeare, critics would have no more difficulty as regards source than they have in dealing with *Othello,* the source for which is just one story. But there was written and performed in England an earlier Hamlet play, usually referred to as the *Ur-Hamlet,* which unfortunately has not survived in manuscript or print.

The *Ur-Hamlet* dates before 1589, for in that year Thomas Nashe made a reference to it. The general opinion is that the *Ur-Hamlet* was the work of Thomas Kyd, best known for the widely popular *The Spanish Tragedy* (printed in 1594), a tragedy containing a ghost and many sensational incidents, in which a father takes vengeance on his son's murderer. A diary entry made by Philip Henslowe, an Elizabethan theatrical manager, tells us that this *Hamlet* was acted on June 11, 1594, by members of the Lord Admiral's Men and the Lord Chamberlain's Men, the latter being the group of which Shakespeare was a member. A third reference is found in Thomas Lodge's *Wit's Misery* (1596).

What conclusions are to be made from all this? First, when Shakespeare's *Hamlet* was originally presented, the audience was already familiar with a Hamlet story, one in which revenge is the dominant theme. Second, since the *Ur-Hamlet* apparently belonged to the popular Senecan tradition of the Elizabethan stage and has been generally attributed to Thomas Kyd, *The Spanish Tragedy,* which survives, must be a prototype. In that play are found the pagan revengeful ghost, the protagonist's unceasing efforts to attain vengeance, his intermittent madness, and considerable sensationalism. Kyd is properly credited with dramatic skill in plot construction, for he carefully provides motivation and suspense before moving to the catastrophe, or resolution. What is missing is the intellectual probing, the apparently studied ambiguity, the complexity of character portrayal, the superior poetry —all of which are to be found in Shakespeare's play. One may assume that the popular *Ur-Hamlet* sufficed insofar as melodrama is concerned; Shakespeare had to transcend the melodramatic, providing the material with new significance and interest, but without sacrificing the sheer excitement of the action.

Stage History

The role of Hamlet has been a prime target of many major actors, and thus the reason for revivals of the play. Richard Burbage, the leading tragedian of Shakespeare's company, played the role in a way which received much public acclaim, as attested by several elegies written on his death in 1619. During the Puritan Interregnum (when the theaters were closed) an abbreviated form, called a droll, was presented; "The Grave-makers," as it was titled, was built around the last act. With the return of the king, the stage revived.

During the Restoration (and carrying into the eighteenth century), most of Shakespeare's plays were "improved" by omissions of unpleasant or allegedly unnecessary material, by additions of comedy or love affairs or music and dancing, and by reversals to happy endings. *Hamlet* endured less change than others; yet it was cut (both to get rid of "irrelevant" matter and to make it conform to usual length), scenes were transposed (supposedly to achieve unity and theatricality), and later a happy ending was added, with Hamlet living and Claudius dying in fight. The most important actor interpreting the role in this period was Thomas Betterton (1635?-1710), the leading member of the Duke's Company.

The role of Hamlet enlisted the efforts of such eighteenth-century tragedians as Robert Wilks (1665?-1732); the great David Garrick (1717-1779), who adapted *Hamlet* at the Drury Lane in 1772 to make it one of his greatest successes; Spranger Barry (1719-1777); John Henderson (1747-1785); and John Kemble (1767-1823) and his brother Charles (1775-1854). A Jubilee, organized by Garrick, was held at Stratford-upon-Avon in September 1769, though weather conditions created problems and curtailed some planned activities. This was the first of the Shakespearean festivals we have come to expect each year in many places throughout the world. Garrick transferred the Jubilee, including scenes from *Hamlet*, to the Drury Lane where it was repeated almost a hundred times. Around the turn of the century John Kemble attempted to restore Shakespeare's text and devised special and more historically accurate costumes, and thus we see the start of a return to study of the play as Shakespeare wrote it.

But in the early nineteenth century Shakespeare was more widely read than acted. Not until William Macready (1793-1873) began to produce the plays in elaborate staging and with full restoration of text (after 1837) was the public offered distinguished Shakespearean theater. Macready also acted the important roles. Charles Kean (1811-1868), like his father Edmund, dominated a production as "star" and carried Kemble's historical staging and costuming to often lampooned extremes. The next star was Henry Irving (1838-1905), the play being tailored to highlight his role. Yet here was also an artist concerned with the integrity of the entire performance, and his 1878 production of *Hamlet* accordingly stands out as a major theatrical accomplishment. Two more end-of-the-century giants must be mentioned: Johnston Forbes-Robertson (1853-1934), who produced *Hamlet* in 1897 with Mrs. Patrick Campbell (1865-1940), and Herbert Beerbohm Tree (1853-1917). Not all these versions, however, allowed the heroic ending we read to take place.

The role of Hamlet even attracted Sarah Bernhardt at the Théâtre Français in mid-century. Foreign productions (including those in America) during the eighteenth and nineteenth centuries were the result of the influence of traveling British troupes. The twentieth century has seen frequent revivals of the play. The way some people today read the play is largely conditioned by whom they saw act in it: John Barrymore (whose "O Vengeance" rang to the ceiling for a full minute), John Gielgud (reflective, intellectual, melancholic), Maurice Evans (a sort of breast-beating—or rather brow-beating—declamation with precise, but inaccurate, articulation), Donald Wolfit (a sympathetic view of a young man troubled by externals), Laurence Olivier (whose 1948 movie was played with obvious Freudian motifs and illogical cinematic settings), and Richard Burton (in a contemporary stage-rehearsal production by Gielgud, in which once in a while characters spoke in character). This latter version was presented in movie houses through "electronovision," and perhaps has become the "standard" for today's generation.

Perhaps no Hamlet, character or play, is going to be satisfactory to all critics and public alike. Most seem to read the play, and thus the title role, in special ways. More than any other play it draws great actors and fiery disagreements. But if nothing else, and regardless of specific production, the viewing of the play as Shakespeare wrote it will impress the audience with its theatricality, its unity, its movement, its great poetry, and even its comedy.

Hamlet as Tragedy

Through the influence of certain plays of the Roman stoic philosopher Seneca (notably *Thyestes)*, an important strand of drama developed in the late sixteenth century: revenge tragedy. Its popularity seems to have begun around 1589 with Thomas Kyd's *The Spanish Tragedy* and to have continued until 1641 with James Shirley's *The Cardinal*. Its ingredients were a son who sought revenge for some wrong (death, deposition) done to his father, a ghost who incited the revenge, a hero who reproached himself for some inability and adopted a pose of madness, crimes of adultery, incest, or murder, intrigue and counterintrigue, and devices such as witches and cemetery scenes. All these conventions, with the exception of witches, are found in some form in *Hamlet*. Nonetheless *Hamlet* is subject to interpretation as "pure tragedy" because the revenge motif is not unquestionably set forth to Hamlet and it does not explain the full conflict which he feels within him.

There are many ways of defining tragedy and thus many tragic elements that may appear in a literary work. Perhaps the simplest definition requires that the protagonist die at the end. However, to make his death significant enough for drama, it was contended that the protagonist should be of noble or important position, for others would then be affected directly by his death. Notions of tragedy developed in the Renaissance from Giovanni Boccaccio's *De Casibus Illustrum Virorum* (Concerning the Fall of Noble Men), through John Lydgate's *The Fall of Princes*. Aristotle's discussion of tragedy was also influential. Hamlet's fall from the noble courtier, described by Ophelia, results in his death and the deaths of Polonius, Rosencrantz, Guildenstern, Ophelia, the queen, Laertes, and the king. The people of Denmark have also suffered because of what happens to Hamlet, and the ruling nobility of Denmark.

Another element which *The Fall of Princes* introduced into the tragic formulas of the Renaissance was that the fall should arise from a shortcoming within the prince: pride, perhaps, or an error of judgment. This idea coincides with Aristotle's statements concerning *hamartia* (popularly known as a tragic flaw, but better translated as an excess of some quality which becomes harmful). The tragic hero was dominated by this weakness and was thus the author of his own misfortune and death, either through action or through inaction. The conflict of the play could arise from the hero's external relationships because of his *hamartia* or from internal struggles to overcome it, or from both.

The most discussed question about *Hamlet* is just what is Hamlet's *hamartia*. There are those who believe it is his inability to act or to make up his mind; there are those who see it as an Oedipus complex or as a death wish. Is his reason submerged by excessive passion? Does he really become temporarily insane? The narrative presenting his story should raise *pathos* (great feeling, suffering) in the audience through their recognition of at least potential elements within themselves or others they know, and *catharsis* (a purging of that pathos) through pity and fear. The play objectifies these feelings and thus eliminates them, which is the psychological definition of catharsis. At the conclusion of the play there should be an uplifting of the spirit if catharsis has taken place. Perhaps, therefore, the sense of a tragic "flaw" in Hamlet that an audience most generally receives is one involving uncertainty through not knowing what is truth, what course of action to take, and what results will ensue upon the action taken.

A more profitable way of looking at *Hamlet* as a tragedy is to perceive the wasting of good (Hamlet) in the process of driving out evil (Claudius). The emphasis, however, is upon the character of evil, not of good. At the moment of tragic vision, the hero comes to recognize the nature of things fully and his relationship to them (as in Act III, Sc. 2); this is called *anagnorisis*. Action then occurs which will both reverse the course of the play and bring an end not fully expected or intended; this is called *peripeteia*. As Hamlet acknowledges Claudius' guilt, he resolves to act. But his actions bring ends unforeseen by him at this time: Polonius' death, Ophelia's death, his own death.

Such ironic results are the foundation of the tragic spirit; they cast a pessimistic gloom over the play until the paradox of good and evil is understood. Hamlet's act *(poiemata)* brings suffering *(pathemata)* but ultimately achieves learning *(mathemata)*, to employ Kenneth Burke's expression of tragic vision.

Summaries and Commentaries by Act and Scene

ACT I • SCENE 1

Summary

The setting is the royal castle at Elsinore. On a platform before the castle, Francisco, a soldier on guard duty, demands the password from Bernardo, an officer, who appears to relieve Francisco at midnight. Francisco expresses his thanks, for it is "bitter cold" and he is "sick at heart." Horatio and Marcellus, who are to join Bernardo in the watch, arrive and identify themselves as loyal Danes. "What, has this thing appear'd tonight?" asks Marcellus, and it is revealed that a strange, frightening apparition was seen during the watch on a previous occasion. Horatio, who has not seen it, has assured Marcellus that it is a hallucination but, at the officer's request, has agreed to join in the watch.

As Bernardo is telling Horatio how the specter had appeared one hour after midnight, the ghost itself enters. It is "like the king that's dead"—that is, it appears in the "fair and warlike form" of the late King Hamlet of Denmark. Marcellus urges Horatio to question it, but when Horatio charges the ghost in heaven's name to speak, the apparition stalks away. The pale and trembling Horatio must agree with Bernardo that it is "something more than fantasy."

In the following discussion, we learn that the ghost has appeared twice before in the same armor King Hamlet wore when he fought the ambitious old Fortinbras, king of Norway, and when he defeated the Poles. Further, in accordance with the solemn agreement made by the two contestants, King Hamlet won Norwegian territory when he defeated and slew his adversary. Now the dead king's son and namesake, young Fortinbras, has raised a force of men willing to fight only for subsistence, and is determined to take back the lands his father lost. Thus, the military preparations and the nightly watch at Elsinore are explained. Bernardo suggests that the ghost's appearance may be a forewarning relating to the war threat, and Horatio recalls the terrifying omens which preceded the assassination of Julius Caesar.

Again the ghost appears, and again Horatio courageously challenges it to speak. But at the crow of a cock, it begins to fade and then disappears. All agree that Hamlet, son of the king whose spirit they may have seen, must be told.

Commentary

First to be noted is the skill with which Shakespeare evokes a mood appropriate to this tragedy. The members of the guard appear in the bitter cold of a northern winter night. Francisco welcomes relief, although his has been a "quiet guard." His feeling of sickness at heart suggests that neither the hour nor the weather explains his uneasiness.

"Long live the king!" exclaims Bernardo, voicing the password when he is challenged by Francisco. "What king?" one asks; and as details relating to Denmark are provided, it seems to be evident that the changing of the guard is symbolic, "a re-enactment of those dynastic changes which frame the play" (H. Levin). Support for such a conclusion is found in Horatio's words when he first addresses the ghost as one "that usurp'st this time of night."

What of the ghost, "this dreaded sight," as Marcellus calls it, which fills Horatio with "fear and wonder?" Some knowledge of Elizabethan and Jacobean ghost-lore is needed. Shakespeare may or may not have believed in ghosts; the characters in this play do, and so did most of his contemporaries, including James I. The prevailing theories were that a ghost might be (1) a hallucination, (2) a spirit returned to perform some deed left undone in life, (3) a specter seen as an omen, (4) a spirit returned from the grave or from purgatory by divine permission, or (5) a devil disguised as a dead person. In the course of the play each of these theories is put to test. Immediately, the first is rejected, but much later in the play it will arise again. The educated, skeptical Horatio proves to his own satisfaction that this particular ghost is a "real" one, not an illusion. Appearing in "warlike form" and as the image of the late King Hamlet, the second may be applicable or, more probably, the third, since Denmark expects an attack led by the young Norwegian prince, Fortinbras. Horatio dwells upon this latter possibility when he speaks of the omens just before Julius Caesar was slain in the Roman Forum.

But Horatio, and members of the guard particularly, fear that the ghost is diabolical. Horatio is called upon to question it because he is a scholar, trained in Latin and knowledgeable in mysterious matters. Among the mortals in this scene, only he is qualified to exorcise an evil spirit. As dawn, heralded by the cock's crow, begins to break and light begins to replace darkness, the ghost "started, like a guilty thing." Marcellus is reminded that, according to a tradition accepted by many, the "bird of dawning singeth all night long" during the Christmas season and then "no spirit dare stir abroad". Indeed this apparition may be a thing of evil.

Significantly, *The Tragedy of Hamlet* is given a Christian setting from the start. Not only is reference made to "our Saviour's birth" in Marcellus' speech, but Horatio uses the proper Christian formula in challenging the ghost: "By heaven I charge thee, speak!"—and his words, according to Marcellus, offend the ghost, which stalks away.

Shakespeare's brilliant opening of *Hamlet* shows the playwright at his best. From the very first words, "Who's there?" an atmosphere of mystery and foreboding is created. The rather prosaic narrative of Horatio, explaining the unusual military preparations, gives our nerves a welcomed opportunity to calm down; then the screw is tightened again with the ghost's second appearance. At the scene's end, Shakespeare has succeeded in planting several tantalizing questions in our minds: Is the ghost the king's ghost? Why has it come back? What message or revelation does it have? And most important, he has turned our attention toward the hero of the play, Prince Hamlet.

ACT I • SCENE 2

Summary

The court mourning for the late King Hamlet is being officially ended and the interest of the audience is maintained by all the fanfare and pageantry of a court entrance, which was loved so much in Shakespeare's day, and long after.

The king and queen being seated, the king makes an impressive speech, apparently expressing his own real sorrow for his brother's death and reconciling it with his swift marriage to his sister-in-law. He thanks his nobility for electing him to the throne and for their support in his arrangements for this swift marriage with his sister-in-law. He passes on quickly to the possible danger presented to the kingdom by the warlike preparations of young Prince Fortinbras of Norway. He has written to Prince Fortinbras' uncle, who has succeeded his brother as King of Norway, to tell him what his young nephew is doing and to get him to stop all this. The old Norwegian king is an invalid, and is not in touch with all that is going on in his own kingdom.

It must be remembered that in all Scandinavian, as well as Teutonic, kingdoms of that early medieval period (the 11th century), the right of succession to a throne had not as yet crystallized upon the eldest son of a monarch. It was still, as it was in England, the right and duty of the great council of chief men to elect the successor from the immediate male relatives of the late ruler. Young Fortinbras had not succeeded to the throne, but his uncle had, just as Hamlet had not been given a chance to present himself for election to the throne before his uncle had obtained the council's acceptance in Denmark.

The king hears Laertes' petition next, not because he is neglecting Hamlet who is of far higher rank, but because the hearing of petitions is next on the agenda, and obviously Hamlet has not made a formal petition. The king is a little extravagant in his willingness to hear Laertes, but it is quite plain that the king feels a very considerable obligation to Polonius, Laertes' father, for his support in his recent election. Upon Polonius giving his rather grudging consent, the king very freely gives Laertes permission to return to live in France.

Now the king turns to Hamlet, who is present in the background still wearing black, in spite of the royal order ending the official mourning period. Claudius does not command him to change his mourning clothes, but he urges him in dignified but hollow phrases to drop this sadness and this mourning costume. Hamlet's mother joins in the attempt at persuasion. Hamlet takes refuge in ironical answers. He does not care what happens to him; he is too heart-broken over his mother's behavior, and over the loss of his father.

His mother tries persuasion again, saying that a father's death is common. He cannot stand this. He breaks out in a passionate declaration of his inward grief for his father, of which this black suit of clothes is merely the outward sign. The king tries again and though his persuasive argument is suspect, his language is dignified, and it is obvious he is going to make every effort to win Hamlet. The king and then the queen urge Hamlet to remain at the court and not go back to Wittenberg. Hamlet consents to his mother's request. Apparently delighted, the king rises and the royal party passes out of the room to celebrate this result with a cannon salute.

Hamlet is left alone, and reveals his inmost thoughts to the audience in this first of his great soliloquies. He feels that he would far rather die than carry on under these conditions. Then he breaks out in an impassioned speech, contrasting his splendid father with this uncle whom he despises. He goes on to a bitter indictment of his mother for her faithlessness to his father's memory. He calls her marriage incestuous.

Horatio, Marcellus and Bernardo interrupt Hamlet's soliloquy. Horatio is specially welcomed by Hamlet as an old friend from the University. When Horatio explains that he came home to be present at the late king's funeral, Hamlet cannot refrain from the bitterly ironical exaggeration, "the funeral baked meats did coldly furnish forth the marriage tables." Horatio, backed by the two others, describes the ghost that they have seen. Hamlet is intensely interested and promises to share their watch that night from before midnight on. When the others leave, in a second soliloquy, he briefly voices his fear that, since his father's spirit comes in armor, there has been some foul play.

Commentary

Claudius, who emerges as the antagonist, is first heard and calls for first attention. It should be obvious that here is no weak individual, but one who is capable and determined. He is fully aware that his marriage to Gertrude is incestuous according to canon law, which is based on the dictum that man and wife become one flesh. He knows further that the marriage, even were it lawful, took place with undue haste. Typically, royal periods of mourning last for a full year; this marriage took place less than two months after the death of Claudius' brother. But this new ruler has taken care to obtain the approval of his court. How he was able to do so in the face of canon law is revealed by his carefully chosen words in the first twenty-five lines of his opening speech, concluding with "So much for him." Notice the skilfully balanced phrases, the careful parallelisms, the antitheses which he employs as he rationalizes his act. Discretion (reason) is set against grief and nature; Gertrude is referred to first as "sometime sister," then as queen, and finally as "imperial jointress" of Denmark. The effect is to convince his audience that he has been motivated by a high sense of public duty.

When he turns to state affairs, Claudius is no less confident, and one must concede that he exhibits decisiveness and capability as a ruler. Although Denmark fears an invasion led by young Fortinbras, the court, and the people in general, may rest assured that their king has taken proper action. King Claudius' public image is a favorable one.

Nor does it appear to diminish when he turns to Hamlet. But again the careful reader will note that, in addressing the prince as "my cousin [kinsman] Hamlet, and my son," Claudius skilfully makes clear the fact that he is in full command and that Hamlet is subject to his pleasure. Once more it is an appeal to reason that seems to color the king's words as he reproves his nephew for undue grief and urges him to embrace forgetfulness. On strict philosophical and religious grounds, his argument is impeccable. All mankind must bow to the inevitable and learn to accept it, for life in general must go on. From this point of view, continued and unhealthy sorrow is indeed "a fault to heaven,/A fault against the dead, a fault to nature".

When Claudius accuses Hamlet of "impious stubbornness," of possessing "A heart unfortified," "a mind impatient" and "An understanding simple and unschool'd," he is saying, in so many words, that the prince lacks the qualities required to rule a kingdom. Thus the king may well intend to strengthen the belief of the Danish counselors that it was best for Claudius to succeed his brother. Certainly the king's words have a rhetorical quality which suggests that he knows that Gertrude and the members of the court also hear his words.

Claudius' call for a celebration with festive drink is, in effect, an order that Hamlet especially, and all others, forget the past and accept the new order. Some commentators (Samuel Johnson, for example) have argued that the king's intemperance, suggested here, is strongly impressed in the play. If this is true, Claudius' appetite for strong drink, according to Renaissance moral philosophy, points to his rejection of reason, which is equated with virtue. But admittedly the evidence to support such a conclusion is rather slight at this stage of the action.

Nothing that Queen Gertrude says or does in this scene informs against her except the fact that she is obviously undisturbed by her new status as wife to Claudius. Her concern for her son seems to be that of a genuinely adoring mother. If Claudius' words tend to arouse suspicions as to his true motives, not so Gertrude's. Her plea, "Let not thy mother lose her prayers, Hamlet," has the ring of sincerity. It is not until one hears the prince speak in soliloquy that Gertrude takes her place, as it were, among the unsympathetic characters. Far more serious than the *haste* of the marriage is the fact that it is incestuous: her marriage to her brother-in-law was a gross violation of the law of the church. Hamlet's indictment of his mother may provide the key to her character—weakness manifested by sensual passion:

Must I remember? Why, she would hang on him
As if increase of appetite had grown
By what it fed on, . . .

Act I, Sc. 2, 143-145

Present also in this scene is Laertes, who speaks just less than
seven lines. He appears as the well-bred son of the Lord Chamberlain,
observing the social graces appropriate to his station and the occasion.
More significant is one's reaction to his father, Polonius, chief counselor to the king, although he speaks just four lines. Just as there is a
contrived element apparent in Claudius' first speech, so there is an artificiality in that of Polonius. The adjective, it has been said, can be the
enemy of the noun. Polonius loves adjectives. Note the pattern of his
discourse: *"slow* leave," *"laboursome* petition," *"hard* consent."
This hardly suggests naturalness or spontaneity.

But the play belongs to Hamlet. Almost everything other characters do or say is relevant primarily to him. His tragedy is already in
progress when he first appears. In this way he provides a contrast to
the usual tragic hero of Renaissance drama, including Shakespeare's
own Othello and Macbeth. Hamlet does not move from a state of well-
being or happiness to adversity and suffering. Nor is his state of un-
happiness attributed to the death of a beloved and honored father;
rather, it is caused by the marriage of his mother to his uncle, who now
is king of Denmark. This is implicit in his first words, an aside. When
Claudius refers to him as cousin and son, the prince remarks bitterly:
"A little more than kin, and less than kind." He is saying that the
uncle-father relationship is monstrous in the literal sense—that is, contrary to the law of nature.

Hamlet's next words are addressed to Claudius and heard by
others. They include a quibble. Do the clouds of grief still hang on
him? No, he is "too much i' th' sun." Clearly, this young prince and
university student has a gift for irony, one which reveals his intellectuality and involves a kind of grim humor. It is quite possible, as some
have suggested, that Hamlet puns upon the word *sun*, since the sun was
often used as a symbol of kingship and the word, of course, is a homo-
nym of *son*. Hamlet may be suggesting here that he stands too closely
to the brightness of the throne, and particularly, to the ceremonial glit-
ter of the moment. Obviously, Hamlet deeply resents Claudius' referring to him as his son. It should be added that those who see *Hamlet*
primarily as an ambition play find here their first evidence that the
tragic hero is motivated by a strong desire to dethrone Claudius and to
rule Denmark.

Much critical attention has been directed to Hamlet's emphatic
use of the word *seems* when his mother asks him, "Why seems it [his
father's death] so particular with thee?", and to his use of the expression *"shows* of grief . . . that a man might *play*." His own feeling

27

"passeth *show*". It has been argued that here Shakespeare develops the theme of appearance versus reality and that he intends to stress Hamlet's dedication to truth in contrast to appearances which serve others, notably Claudius. Certainly he is presented as a disruptive figure in this assembly, and his "inky cloak" and suit of "solemn black" provide a telling criticism of Claudius and Gertrude. Others may act a part, making use of "windy suspiration of forc'd breath" (sighing) and "fruitful river in the eye" (weeping); Hamlet is incapable of such posturing.

As has been stated above, the overwhelming cause of Hamlet's grief is revealed in his soliloquy: the incestuous union of his mother and his uncle. Since the doctrine involved here is not a current one, and indeed was not universal when Shakespeare wrote *Hamlet,* some explanation is desirable. That marriage between a man and his dead brother's wife not only took place, but also was sometimes legally authorized before and after Shakespeare wrote the play is undeniable. But according to the canonical law implicit in Shakespeare's play, such a marriage is strictly forbidden. That law is based upon the sacramental view of a mystical bond formed in marriage which creates a relationship between man and wife as close as that which exists between blood relations. From the religious point of view, which cannot be ignored if one is to do justice to Shakespeare's intentions, the marriage of Claudius and Gertrude is, to use the official language of the period, "incestuous and unlawful and altogether null and void." One wonders why the subjects of the king and queen voiced no protest or expressed no feeling of shock. But for the poet-dramatist's purpose, it is enough that the young, idealistic Christian prince should believe that the honor of the Danish royal family has been stained. It may be added that, traditionally, incest was considered to be an offense against the whole of society. If that view is applicable in Shakespeare's play, then Hamlet has a public duty to oppose Claudius, and the issue is not merely a personal or domestic one.

So great is Hamlet's grief that, if not for the religious injunction against suicide, that ultimate act of despair and mortal sin, he would take his own life: "O, that this too too sullied flesh would melt," he exclaims.

Here, then, is the crushing discovery of great evil by a young idealist. Little wonder that his world has become "stale, flat, and unprofitable." The metaphor Hamlet uses is fitting: his world has become an "unweeded garden." Elsewhere in Shakespeare's plays, notably in *Richard II,* garden and weed imagery is used for the development of theme. The properly tended garden represents an orderly world; weeds represent disease or corruption which destroys order.

Consistent with this outlook, Hamlet identifies his dead father with Hyperion in comparison to Claudius, who is likened to a satyr. Hyperion, or Apollo, was the god of light, and light traditionally has been equated with order and virtue. A satyr is something of a goatish caricature of a human being, and has attained the secondary meaning of "lecherous man." For Hamlet, lust, not love, determines the relationship between Claudius and Gertrude. According to the moral philosophy of the Renaissance, lust was viewed as evidence of degeneracy, involving the rejection of God-given reason. The Prince now sees his mother as incapable of love, for he refers to her earlier regard for King Hamlet in terms of physical appetite. Most devastating is his indictment:

> O, most wicked speed, to post
> With such dexterity to incestuous sheets!
>
> > (Act I, Sc. 2, 156-57)

In this soliloquy, Hamlet demonstrates his considerable ability to move from particulars to generalization. If a mother and wife who appeared so loving can so degrade herself, then all women, all daughters of Eve, are immoral: "Frailty, thy name is woman!"

Facing this tormenting situation, Hamlet says that he "must hold [his] tongue"—that is, he can do nothing. But perhaps some indication that he is called upon to act has been provided. Claudius, he declares, is no more like his royal brother than Hamlet himself is like Hercules. The prince's low estimation of his own abilities may suggest that, previously uncalled upon to prove himself, he soon will face a task which, in its way, will be as challenging as any of the labors of Hercules.

"I am glad to see you well," says Hamlet automatically when Horatio greets him, interrupting his thoughts. But then he is all graciousness and warmth when he recognizes his friend and fellow-student. Some have seen Hamlet's reaction to Horatio either as a sudden change in mood (which is an early indication of emotional instability caused by excessive grief) or merely as an effort on Hamlet's part to control himself. But it may be more reasonable to conclude that, for the first of many times in this play, Shakespeare provides a glimpse of Hamlet's normal self—the Hamlet before his tragedy began, as it were.

The mention of the funeral provokes Hamlet's grimly witty replies. Surely Horatio has returned to attend the wedding of Hamlet's mother for which "The funeral bak'd-meats/Did coldly furnish forth the marriage tables" (180-81). However high-spirited, these words reveal that his mood has changed back to that of profound melancholy. Quite naturally he evokes mentally the image of his father, and quite naturally Horatio is startled. The transition to Horatio's report of what he and the guard have seen is thus skilfully achieved. Before proceeding, however, one should not ignore Hamlet's tribute to his father. In the soliloquy, the late king was identified with a Greek god; here Hamlet does not depend upon the language of the scholar and, if anything, pays greater homage: "He was a man, take him for all in all,/I

29

shall not look upon his like again" (187-88). Note the emphasis on a *man*, a *human* being, not "a beast, that wants discourse of reason." In both *King Lear* and *Macbeth,* two of the four great Shakespearean tragedies which include *Hamlet,* the dramatist uses the word *man* in this sense. The implications with reference to Claudius, who now rules Denmark and calls himself Hamlet's father, are evident.

It is an excited prince who cross-examines Horatio, Marcellus, and Bernardo: "Where was this? . . . Did you not speak to it? . . . Arm'd, say you? . . . Stay'd it long? There follows the expression of determination to "watch to-night" and his insistence that they tell no one else what they have seen. Perhaps there is significance in Hamlet's question, "Then saw you not his [not *its*] face?" At this point, the question may indicate that the prince is sure that the ghost is "honest," not a "goblin damn'd;" later he will not be so sure. To be noted also is the fact that Horatio reports that the ghost appeared "more in sorrow than in anger," a statement that is contrary to his earlier observation.

The words that Hamlet speaks when alone at the end of this scene suggest, first, that he now considers the possibility of the apparition's being an omen of evil; and, second, that he suspects some "foul play."

ACT I • SCENE 3

Summary
This scene brings us into the midst of a family who may be considered typical of the best that this court of Denmark has to offer.

Laertes, in the manner of an experienced older brother, takes it upon himself to instruct his sister in the ways of the world and particularly as to her behavior in it. He warns her against Hamlet and his attention. He judges Hamlet by his own man-about-town standards and cannot imagine that a prince in Hamlet's position could have any purity of motive. He warns her that Hamlet is not exactly his own master in deciding whom he shall marry, but would have to consult the council. Further he warns her that she is in danger of loss of reputation even in the most innocent dealings with Hamlet. Ophelia demurely hears the long, wordy lecture through. When Laertes finishes his enlightening speech, Ophelia whimsically hopes that he will at least follow his own advice. Laertes, thrown off balance, suddenly remembers that he has pressing business elsewhere. The entry of Polonius stops his hasty exit and he is subjected, in front of Ophelia, to a similar lecture from his father of about the same length as the one to which he has just subjected his sister. This one is much more of a masterpiece of the same man-about-town morality. Its whole tenor is, "Don't ever commit yourself." Find out who the best people are before you make any friends. Keep out of quarrels, but if you can't help getting into one, give a good account of yourself. Listen to everyone but don't agree with anybody and don't promise anything. Don't dress flashily, but don't be careless about your dress. Don't borrow money and don't lend money; either way you'll lose a friend.

Now it's Polonius' turn with Ophelia. Polonius goes over the same ground about her relations with Hamlet as Laertes has done and winds up by forbidding her to see Hamlet any more. In the manner of the daughters of that day she promises to obey, and we fear she will.

Commentary

In this scene one meets Polonius and his family at home and learns much about each member, particularly the son and father. Moreover, a new story element is introduced—Hamlet's apparent love for Ophelia.

How does Laertes appear? On the one hand, he seems to be the devoted brother quite rightly concerned with protecting his sister; he also seems to be the dutiful son who accords his father proper respect. But in the total of fifty-three lines of blank verse which constitute Laertes' lecture on sisterly conduct, the note of artificiality and lack of spontaneity come through strongly. This is the contrived style of the young courtier, with a succession of metaphors, studied parallelisms, and antitheses. Taken together with Polonius' advice to his son and his words to his daughter, Laertes' lines suggest a limitation in regard to the family's concept of honor.

Polonius' lines are even more revealing. His advice to Laertes (Act I, Sc 3, 59-80) comprises one of the very well-known passages in the play. Although some early commentators took the lord chamberlain's words to be evidence of profound wisdom, the consensus is that the elderly lord chamberlain is merely parroting copybook maxims familiar to any Elizabethan schoolboy. His lines reveal a vain and limited character. As one informed critic (H. Levin) has pointed out, most of what Polonius tells his son relates to etiquette, not ethics. This father is coaching his son in how to "act," how to "seem," how to "show" himself publicly. Yet his final precept is ethical, not practical wordly counsel:

This above all: to thine own self be true,
And it must follow as the night the day
Thou canst not then be false to any man.
(Act I, Sc. 3, 77-79)

Climaxing his rather long speech, this change of tone can only be taken ironically.

If this unfavorable view of Polonius seems to be unduly harsh at this early stage of the action, consider his questions and remarks to Ophelia, who dutifully reports that Hamlet has "made many tenders/Of his affection" but has done so in honorable fashion. Polonius flatly rejects the possibility of sincere affection; he is convinced that

"the holy vows of heaven" are no more than snares to entrap the innocent and unwary. He seems to take positive delight in his off-color
interpretation of Hamlet's recent interest in his daughter. Most dam-
aging is his warning:

> Tender yourself more dearly,
> Or (not to crack the wind of the poor phrase,
> Running it thus) you'll tender me a fool.
>
> (Act I, Sc. 3, 107-9)

Vanity and suspicion come through strongly in this passage. Polonius
appears to be much more concerned about his public image than about
the welfare of his daughter. Again, his emphasis is upon how one
should play a role, how one should act, show, seem.

One other significant point is made clear in this scene, one relating
to the status of Hamlet. He is not a *private* individual but a *public* one;
what he does has public, not merely personal, import. This Laertes
says:

> His greatness weighed, his will is not his own.
> For he himself is subject to his birth.
> He may not, as unvalued persons do,
> Carve for himself, for on his choice depends
> The safety and health of this whole state, . . .
>
> (Act I, Sc. 3, 17-21)

This is the first passage which has been cited to support the argument
that Hamlet unmistakably has the duty to avenge his father's death
and to do so without delay.

ACT I • SCENE 4

Summary

Hamlet appears on the sentry-walk high on the battlements with
Horatio and Marcellus just before midnight. The nervous tension is
apparent from the comments on the cold and the asking for the time.
Their attention is suddenly diverted to the noises of celebration in the
castle below. These sounds of gaiety lead Hamlet into a denunciation
of the national custom of excessive drinking which, he says, has won
his countrymen an unenviable reputation abroad for drunkenness. He
goes on to philosophize on the fact that one defect of manners or character can ruin a lifetime of high achievement.

Just then the ghost enters. For a second Hamlet is taken off his
guard. But almost immediately he addresses it and tries to learn the
reason for its appearance. The ghost merely beckons Hamlet to follow
it.

It must be remembered that the paralyzing fear that a ghost might be a malignant spirit of Satan was common. Hence, the frantic concern of Horatio and Marcellus that Hamlet should not follow the ghost for fear it was merely going to lure him over the battlements to the crags and the sea below. Hamlet, though not ignorant of the cause of their fear, insists on following. They seek to restrain him but he breaks from them, threatening death to any who would restrain him further.

His friends follow him at a distance to see that he does not come to harm. Marcellus makes the since-famous remark, "Something is rotten in the State of Denmark." This is the second of these open predictions of impending misfortune. Hamlet voices the first one in Scene 2: "All is not well./I doubt some foul play."

Commentary

Once more, setting and mood are provided economically in broken lines of blank verse and informal diction. It is very close to midnight, the hour when the spirit appeared on the previous occasion.

Hamlet's "dram of evil" speech (14-38) is of special interest and possibly of major importance. Inspired as it is by his reaction to the sound of drunken revelry coming from the court where Claudius fulfills his pledge to celebrate what he earlier called Hamlet's "gentle and unforc'd accord", the prince again demonstrates his ability to move from particulars to generalization. Excessive drinking, encouraged now by the king himself, leads other nations to use the "swinish phrase" *drunkards* when speaking of the Danes; in the same way, Hamlet concludes, a fault in an individual may override his virtues and lead to his downfall.

Many commentators argue, understandably, that the subject of Hamlet's discourse is specifically the reputation of Claudius, who now rules Denmark but who, according to Hamlet, is no more like his predecessor than is Hyperion to a satyr. The king's taking "his rouse" may also serve to illustrate the deterioration of Elsinore since the death of King Hamlet. Moreover, his speech may be intended to illustrate the prince's propensity for thought; those who accept the Romantic view of a Hamlet made incapable of positive action by this very tendency find no more in the "dram of evil" speech than an example of this trait.

But a sufficient number of distinguished Shakespeareans consider Hamlet to be a superior individual who, nevertheless, becomes a slave of passion. To them, these lines incorporate an exploration of the problem of good and evil (the problem basic to tragedy) and may well provide the key to the Hamlet mystery. Their views deserve notice.

When one hears Hamlet speak of the "o'ergrowth of some complexion," "the stamp of one defect," corruption from a "particular fault" leading to the corruption of an individual "as pure as grace" in other ways, the inclination is to believe that Shakespeare is underscoring a significant theme. Hamlet provides three possible answers to the problem of evil—three reasons why there may be present "some vicious mole of nature" which may lead to general disapproval and downfall. The first one is inherited defect, which obviously does not involve human responsibility, the individual being a victim of fate ("fortune's star"). If that were the answer in *Hamlet*, then the play could not be classified as Renaissance high tragedy, but rather as one based on, or consistent with, Medieval theory, according to which individual choice and responsibility do not exist.

The second answer involves the "o'ergrowth of some complexion" which often breaks "down the pales and forts of reason." Here human responsibility is evident. Some knowledge of Renaissance moral theory relating to "complexions" is required if one is to understand Hamlet's words. At the simplest literal level, the term *complexion* may be defined as "natural quality." But for Shakespeare's generation, it had a more specific meaning. It referred to a person's temperament resulting from the supposed combination of four bodily fluids, called humors. The complexions were sanguine, melancholic, choleric, and phlegmatic. Proper balance of the humors in the body made possible the healthy individual; an excess or deficiency of one humor led to a psychological or physical imbalance. According to this theory, so widely accepted in the Elizabethan and Jacobean ages, the intellectual was especially susceptible to melancholy. This passion of excessive brooding negated the powers of reason and thus the ability to act positively. Those who see Hamlet as the victim of excessive grief which causes him to delay or to act only on impulse find here support for this theory. That the prince himself should provide support for such a theory is not surprising: his intellectual superiority is well established in the play and, on more than one occasion he emerges as the best critic of himself.

The third answer is that relating to "some habit that too much o'erleavens [mixes with]/The form of plausive [pleasing] manners." Excessive drink obviously is one such habit, and it is the one which Hamlet must have in mind, in view of the merriment which motivates his speech. Such a habit, like the "o'ergrowth of some complexion," may lead an individual, however virtuous he may appear to be in other respects, to reject reason, the quality which distinguishes him from the beast. It will be recalled that Hamlet uses bestial imagery in referring to the drunken revelry, speaking of how the "kettledrum and trumpet thus bray out" and of the "swinish phrase" used to describe those prone to excessive drinking. Obviously, the charge of brutish behavior could be applicable only to Claudius. But Hamlet himself is deeply concerned with public reputation and certainly with the honor of his family. One need not fear that he will be guilty of indulging a bad habit leading to the rejection of reason. If any of the answers to the problem of evil which he advances turn out to be applicable to him, it must be either adverse fate or uncontrolled passion that is to blame.

"Angels and ministers of grace defend us!" exclaims Hamlet as he sees the apparition for the first time, voicing the orthodox Christian formula to be used on such a terrifying occasion. Consistent with contemporary ideas relating to ghosts, he knows that it may be "a spirit of health" (one divinely allowed to return to accomplish a rightful mission) or a "goblin damn'd" (an evil spirit, a devil, or even Satan himself) appearing in the form and dress of King Hamlet and intent on leading Hamlet to destruction—perhaps to draw him into madness, as Horatio warns. But Hamlet makes a positive identification of the ghost as "King, father; royal Dane." He assumes that the spirit has come from the grave where the body of King Hamlet, in "the very armour he had on/When he th' ambitious Norway combated," (Act I, Sc. 1, 60-62) had been buried.

Despite argument and attempts to restrain him physically, the prince obeys the summons of the ghost. What if his life be threatened? Having listened to him voice his innermost thoughts, one knows that he does not value life in a world where traditional virtues no longer flourish.

ACT I • SCENE 5

Summary

The ghost tells Hamlet that it is the spirit of his father, doomed for a time to walk on earth during the nights and to endure purgatorial fires during daytime as punishment for sins committed during life. The ghost calls upon him to prove his love for his father: "Revenge his foul and most unnatural murder." Hamlet is told that although King Hamlet's death was attributed to the sting of a serpent, it was Claudius, "that incestuous, that adulterate beast," who murdered his brother. The prince receives this startling news as if it were confirmation of his suspicions. The ghost then fills in the details. The treacherous Claudius poured poison into the ear of the sleeping King Hamlet, sending him to his death without sacraments, and then won the affections of Queen Gertrude, thus depriving him at once "Of life, of crown, of queen." No longer must Denmark be ruled by the incestuous murderer; Hamlet is called upon to kill his uncle. But the ghost adds a word of caution: the son is not to contaminate himself by seeking to punish his mother; he is to leave her punishment to heaven and to her own conscience. "Hamlet, remember me," says the ghost as it departs. The prince solemnly vows to wipe away all else from his memory except that which the ghost has told him.

It is a highly excited Hamlet who answers the calls of Horatio and Marcellus. His replies to their questions are evasive. When he calls upon the two to take an oath of secrecy regarding what they have seen this night, the voice of the ghost is heard repeatedly from below the platform. Hamlet moves wildly about the platform, now addressing the ghost, now calling upon his friends to place their hands upon his sword and take the oath. In a more restrained mood, the prince enlarges the conditions of the oath. If he chooses to pretend to be mentally deranged, they are not to give the slightest indication that they know the reason for his behavior. Again the ghost's voice is heard: "Swear." When the oath is taken, Hamlet, now subdued, thanks his friends and then expresses his sense of the heaviness of the burden he now carries.

Commentary

One of the prime concerns of the ghost is that, as a mortal, it was denied the opportunity to be shriven (receive absolution for sins prior to death) and thus must endure spiritual purgation before it can be admitted to heaven. But what of the "foul crimes" admitted to have been committed by King Hamlet, the man whom his son so much reveres? Obviously he was not perfect; no mortal is, according to church doctrine because mankind remains tainted as the result of original sin. The ghost is only too aware of mortal imperfections; it has a conscience practically Calvinistic in its strictness.

Hamlet will later have doubts about the nature of the ghost, although they will be dispelled. But some Shakespearean commentators remain uncertain that Hamlet's doubts have been dispelled, and their view should not be ignored. It has been pointed out that a repentant spirit from purgatory would not appear as an armed warrior even if its mortal body had been so outfitted for burial. But since the ghost's mission is to call upon Hamlet to attack Claudius, who now rules an armed Denmark, its military costume is held to be the proper one. One may add that it is most effective theatrically.

Nevertheless, a degree of uncertainty remains. When the ghost warns Hamlet against failure to execute revenge, it employs a simile which is rather strained, especially for a Christian spirit from purgatory, not from the pagan underworld or Elysium:

And duller shouldst thou be than the fat weed
That rots itself in ease on Lethe wharf,
Wouldst thou not stir in this.

(Act I, Sc. 5, 32-34)

Lethe, it will be recalled, is the Greek mythological river of Hades whose waters, when drunk, caused forgetfulness of the past. To be sure, much Renaissance poetry is filled with a mixture of pagan and Christian elements. Yet one recalls that the ghost "started like a guilty thing" when the cock crew at daybreak (Act I, Sc. 1, 148 ff.). Is this the reaction of a Christian spirit? But it must be conceded that in the present scene the ghost's behavior never suggests guilt. To Hamlet it says, "But soft! methinks I scent the morning air./Brief let me be." In the earlier scene, dawn began to break before the Ghost, unable to speak its words to the proper person, was aware that its allotted time was up. When Horatio reported what he had seen, he said only that "it shrunk in haste" away. His earlier words were natural enough under the circumstances; they emphasized his uncertainty and fright.

The climax of the ghost's recital is reached after just twenty-two lines:

> If thou didst ever thy dear father love—
> . . .
> Revenge his foul and most unnatural murder.
>
> (Act I, Sc. 5, 23, 25)

The two major issues basic to Hamlet's tragedy are now joined: the murder of a king and father, and the marriage of Claudius and Gertrude. The murder of a king, especially, is foul and unnatural because he is God's minister on earth, so loyal Elizabethans and Jacobeans fervently believed. The ghost denounces Claudius as "that incestuous, that adulterate beast" and speaks of Gertrude as that "seeming-virtuous queen." Hamlet is implored not to let "the royal bed of Denmark be/A couch for luxury [sensuality] and damned incest" (82-83). The adultery and incest, which concern the ghost quite as much as does the murder by means of "leperous distilment," may simply refer to the marriage. Whether or not Gertrude was unfaithful prior to the death of King Hamlet remains a disputed point. But one thing is clear: Prince Hamlet is not alone in his revulsion, unless this ghost is indeed a "goblin damn'd," intent upon leading the young prince to destruction—or unless one takes the unusual and radical view that Hamlet, separated from his companions on the platform, is the victim of a hallucination and that the ghost is actually voicing Hamlet's own thoughts. If this is indeed "an honest ghost," its concern for the purity of "the royal bed of Denmark," as well as the crown, suggests that Hamlet is being called upon to execute public justice, not private revenge. Yet this spirit remains curiously tender in its attitude toward Gertrude:

> Taint not thy mind, nor let thy soul contrive
> Against thy mother aught. Leave her to heaven. . . .
>
> (Act I, Sc. 5, 85-86)

In a state of great excitement, Hamlet declares himself ready to seek revenge. He declares this even before the identification of the murderer is made and the details of the crime are provided, although it is reasonable to conclude that he could suspect no one but Claudius. The figurative language which he uses to emphasize his determination deserves attention. He will sweep to his revenge "with wings as swift/As meditation or the thoughts of love." The simile is appropriate for a young university scholar and a lover, and Hamlet has been established as both. But does prompt execution of an action involve meditation? In the present circumstances, does it not call for unquestioned, dutiful acceptance of the execution of blood-revenge, an eye for an eye, a tooth for a tooth? Blood-revenge is based on the barbarous *lex talionis*, the primitive law of the blood feud, whereby the nearest of kin is bound to avenge the victim by slaying his murderer. Is Shakespeare, then, restricted by his source or sources, including the original thirteenth century version by Saxo Grammaticus? Or has he intentionally complicated Hamlet's problem in his play for which he provided a Christian framework?

The ghost's injunction, "Remember me," spoken just before its exit becomes for Hamlet an obsession. From the cellarage, the ghost repeats the command to "Swear" after Horatio and Marcellus rejoin the distracted prince. Emotionally, most audiences and readers accept the ghost as "a spirit of health," just as Hamlet does in this scene. But, if only in afterthought, it remains a puzzling, disturbing thing. It may be relevant, in this connection, that the cellarage (which term gives this scene its usual name) was the cavernous area under the Elizabethan stage which was popularly called "hell."

"Come on. You hear this fellow in the cellarage," says Hamlet to Horatio and Marcellus. A few critics wonder if the two friends did hear the ghost, although Horatio immediately replies, "Propose the oath, my lord." Although he comes close to revealing the ghost's testimony to his friends, Hamlet does not do so. Both Horatio and Marcellus prove their loyalty to him by taking the solemn oath not to reveal what they have *seen*.

Much has been written about Hamlet's decision to feign madness, "To put an antic disposition on." Some commentators are content to observe that the hero's pose of madness is basic to the original story of Hamlet and must have been included in the pre-Shakespearean *Ur-Hamlet*, and to conclude that audiences expected the hero to feign madness. But such an answer does not suffice for those who refuse to believe that Shakespeare permitted himself to be rigidly bound by his source or that he catered to popular taste in this play. Perhaps Hamlet's own words and behavior, after he was joined by his friends, suggested to him the adoption of the antic disposition; clearly he knew that the shock of discovery made impossible normal behavior:

> The time is out of joint. O cursed spite
> That ever I was born to set it right.
>
> (Act I, Sc. 5, 188-89)

For Goethe, who envisioned Hamlet as a delicate soul unequal to the performance of the great task laid upon him, these two lines proved the "key to Hamlet's whole procedure" (*Wilhelm Meister,* 1778). Later critics, most of whom do not accept the Romantic interpretation of the prince's character, nevertheless agree that these are indeed key lines. The ghost warns Hamlet not to taint his mind by seeking to punish Gertrude. Can he, however, kill his uncle-king without his mind becoming tainted?

ACT II • SCENE 1

Summary

At his home, Polonius instructs Reynaldo to journey to Paris and to give Laertes money and messages. Reynaldo is also given detailed instructions on how to find out if Laertes is behaving himself. Reynaldo is to seek out other Danes in Paris, ones who are sure to know Laertes, and to obtain all the gossip relating to him.

Ophelia enters in a state of fright. She tells Polonius that Hamlet has come to her, his clothes in disarray, his face lacking of color, the very picture of despair. Her father promptly diagnoses Hamlet's condition: the prince suffers from love-madness brought on by Ophelia's refusal to accept his attention in accordance with her father's instructions. Polonius now believes that he should not have been so strict in this affair. He will inform the king of what he has just learned.

Commentary

The late T. S. Eliot found nothing relevant in this scene as far as the instructions to Reynaldo are concerned. Others have argued that it is included only to convey the sense of stagnation in Elsinore, for much time has elapsed since Laertes' departure and Hamlet's encounter with the ghost. Surely there is much more to be said in justification of this scene.

Earlier the statement was made that this is Hamlet's play and that almost everything any other character says or does relates in some way to him. Polonius is the leading courtier at Elsinore and chief adviser to King Claudius. Already certain limitations in his character have been revealed—the artificiality of his discourse, an inclination toward cynicism and suspicion of other people's motives, and a self-confidence amounting to vanity. This portrait of the lord chamberlain, whose major concern earlier was that Ophelia's behavior might "tender [him] a fool" is now no less concerned that Laertes' conduct in Paris does not make him look bad. In his worldliness and cynicism, he is absolutely sure that he knows how young men behave when away from parental control—drinking, fencing, quarreling, and woman-hunting. Reynaldo, Polonius says, is to let Laertes "ply his music"—that is, keep a close eye on him and let him reveal his secrets. Not only is Polonius ready to believe the worst about his son, but he also seems to be incapable of honesty in his methods. His outlook and conduct suggest the kind of world in which Hamlet is now living. Indirection—espionage—becomes an elaborate game very soon in this play; this episode prepares the way for it.

The second episode in this scene is concerned with Ophelia's report to her father. From her description of Hamlet, his clothes in disarray, "Pale as his shirt, his knees knocking each other," it is obvious that he has adopted the "antic disposition." But when Ophelia says that he appeared

> . . . with a look so piteous in purport
> As if he had been loosed out of hell
> To speak of horrors. . . .
>
> (Act II, Sc. 1, 82-84)

one inevitably recalls the ghost's revelations. This and other details relating to Hamlet's distress suggest that more is involved here than assumed madness.

Hamlet has chosen to appear before Ophelia, who refused to accept his letters or to let him talk to her, as the courtly lover suffering from love-sickness. It is inconceivable that Hamlet would indulge in such posturing even if Ophelia's rejection of his attentions were a crushing blow. Perhaps, as some critics believe, those "tenders of affection" of which Ophelia spoke earlier may have been made by Hamlet in order to test the validity of his own generalization: "Frailty, thy name is woman!" It will be recalled that in the same soliloquy he had declared that all "uses of this world" had become for him "weary, stale, flat, and unprofitable." This hardly suggests that he was in the mood for love. But this is not to deny that Hamlet was attracted to Ophelia. The essential point is this: if one is to do justice to Hamlet's status as a tragic hero who rejects "seeming," it must not be assumed that he now appears as a sentimental pretender. Adopting the "antic disposition" is something else again. In this world of Elsinore, where Polonius is established as the wisest counselor, the prince must meet indirection with indirection. Claudius must not learn what Hamlet intends; let his lord chamberlain report that his nephew suffers only from love-madness.

Polonius' reaction is, of course, predictable. With complete self-confidence, he declares that Hamlet suffers from "the very ecstasy of love." It may be argued that his decision to report to Claudius what he has learned is a proper one under the circumstances, and that he really believes the well-being not only of Hamlet but also of Queen Gertrude to be involved. But when one recalls his prime concern with his own reputation, rather than with the welfare of his daughter, the inclination is to see him as being anxious chiefly to prove how wise he is.

ACT II • SCENE 2

Summary

In the castle, the king, accompanied by his queen, welcomes Rosencrantz and Guildenstern, who have obeyed his summons to court. Claudius speaks of Hamlet's strange behavior and asks these two friends of the Prince to see if they can find out the reason. The queen adds her request that they do so. Showing their respect for royal authority, both agree to do their utmost to learn the cause of Hamlet's affliction. The king and queen express their gratitude, and the two young men leave.

Polonius enters and announces the return of Cornelius and Voltimand, who were sent as ambassadors to Norway. When Claudius thanks him as "the father of good news," the lord chamberlain takes the opportunity to inform the king that he has found the "very cause of Hamlet's lunacy." Claudius urges him to speak of that, but Polonius suggests that the king first receive his ambassadors.

Voltimand is the one who makes the report to Claudius. The elderly and ailing king of Norway has restrained his nephew Fortinbras. Instead of moving against Denmark, the latter agrees to lead his troops against the Poles. The Norwegian ruler asks that Fortinbras be given permission to pass through Danish territory. Claudius expresses his pleasure in hearing the report and states that he will reply to the request after giving it full consideration.

Polonius now begins his speech in an elaborate, wordy manner. Hamlet, he declares, is infatuated with Ophelia, in proof whereof he reads a love letter written by the prince partly in highly artificial prose, partly in rhymed lines which never approach poetry. He then provides details relating to Hamlet and Ophelia and concludes that he has indeed found the source and cause of the prince's illness. After all, he reminds his listeners, has he ever been found in error when the king has asked him to express his firm opinion? Both Claudius and Gertrude agree that love-madness may indeed explain Hamlet's behavior, but the cautious king wants additional proof. Polonius is ready with a plan. He will let Ophelia meet the prince; the king and Polonius will conceal themselves and observe the encounter. At his request, the royal couple and their attendants leave just after Hamlet enters, reading a book, thus giving Polonius a chance to find out what he can from the young prince.

In his answers to Polonius' questions, Hamlet convinces Polonius that he is indeed the victim of unrequited love. Actually his own questions and his responses openly ridicule Polonius. Furthermore, he tacitly warns the lord chamberlain that Ophelia's virtue is in jeopardy, and he expresses his own wish for death. Still convinced that he has diagnosed Hamlet's condition accurately, Polonius nevertheless is impressed by what he calls "method" (basic sense) in the prince's madness.

When Polonius leaves, Rosencrantz and Guildenstern enter. Hamlet greets them cordially as his "excellent good friends." Yet in the verbal exchange which follows, he becomes increasingly sardonic and suspicious of the motives of these two. Finally he succeeds in making them admit that they had been instructed by the king and queen to seek him out and to observe him carefully. The prince then tells them what to report to their majesties: he has lost his mirth and given up most normal activities because the universe, which he believed to be wondrous, now appears to him to be foul; and man, the so-called paragon of the animals, no longer delights him—nor does woman either. The two then remark that, in his present mood, the prince will not enjoy the performance of the actors who have just arrived in Elsinore. But Hamlet immediately shows his interest, especially in "He that plays the king."

Learning that these are "the tragedians of the city" whose performances have previously pleased him, Hamlet asks why they are travelling. He is told that an acting company of children have engaged in an attack upon the "common plays" and that theatrical performances by the adult companies have been suspended, popular fancy having turned to the child actors. The prince then tells Rosencrantz and Guildenstern that they, like the actors, are welcome; but he adds that Claudius and Gertrude are deceived about his madness.

Polonius returns to announce the arrival of the players. Hamlet promptly resumes the antic pose, the whole time baiting the elderly lord chamberlain. Then, when four or five players enter, he greets them warmly and shows a keen interest in, and knowledge of, the theater. At Hamlet's request, the first player recites a set speech from a play based on Aeneas' tale to Dido as told in Virgil's *Aeneid*, one which Hamlet describes as excellent but lacking popular appeal. The speech, which is in epic style, tells of the slaying of King Priam by Pyhrrus, son of Achilles. After requesting Polonius to see to it that the players are well housed, Hamlet speaks in private to the first player. It is arranged that on the next day the acting company will present a play called *The Murder of Gonzago,* the script of which will include some twelve to sixteen lines provided by Hamlet.

Alone, Hamlet again voices his innermost thoughts. First, he expresses wonder that a player could so realistically portray grief over the death of a character in dramatic fiction. He himself has genuine cause for passion, yet what has he done? Bitterly he denounces himself for failing to take action against Claudius; he accuses himself of laziness, cowardice, even villainy. Suddenly he interrupts himself and acknowledges that he has been indulging in pointless anger. He then reveals his intentions in having the players enact *The Murder of Gonzago* before the king and the assembled court. During the performance he will keep his eyes on Claudius who, if guilty, will surely flinch and thus inadvertently prove that the ghost spoke true words. However convinced he had been that it was an "honest" spirit when he listened to its words, Hamlet now is not sure; perhaps it is the devil who has used his power "to assume a pleasing shape" in order to lead the prince to damnation.

Commentary

On the surface, Claudius appears gracious, genuinely solicitous about his nephew's well-being, and competent as a ruler in his attention to state affairs. No one should underestimate his capabilities, and these include positive action. Threats against the crown coming from abroad can be and are met; Cornelius and Voltimand report that Fortinbras will not invade Denmark. But the threat to Claudius in Hamlet's behavior remains. The intensity of the king's concern is evident, especially when the confident Polonius assures him that he has "found/The very cause of Hamlet's lunacy." He exclaims, "O, speak of that; that I do long to hear." Gertrude is sufficiently concerned; but it is Claudius, not she, who speaks of Hamlet's madness. Only at Polonius' urging does the king agree to see his ambassadors before exploring that subject. It will be noted that the queen is not convinced that her son suffers from love-madness:

> I doubt it is no other but the main,
> His father's death and our o'erhasty marriage.
> (Act II, Sc. 2, 56-57)

When Claudius tells Rosencrantz and Guildenstern about Hamlet's "transformation," he says that neither "th' exterior nor the inward man/Resembles that it was." Recalling the falseness and flattery in Claudius' first speech in this play, one may find evidence of Machiavellianism here. Claudius is quite aware of how appearances may deceive—how it is possible to seem, to act a part.

If this generalization on the basis of one brief passage seems to be unwarranted, consider how readily Claudius approves of Polonius' underhanded methods and remains undisturbed by the unsavory terms in which the lord chamberlain speaks of them. Polonius refers to hunting the "trail of policy" and says that he will "loose" Ophelia to Hamlet. The prince, apparently, is the prey of hunters, and poor Ophelia is to be cast in the role of a hound. The king's use of the word *sift* ("Well, we shall sift him") is good Elizabethan English, but its connotation here is as unpleasant as are the phrases used by Polonius.

In their interview with the king and queen, Rosencrantz and Guildenstern present themselves as dutiful subjects of the crown, willing to serve when called upon. Although their supposed concern for Hamlet's well-being is not expressed until the end of this episode, they also appear to be loyal friends of the prince. Yet the very way in which their concern is expressed arouses some suspicions: "Heavens make our presence and our practices/Pleasant and helpful to him!" Perhaps the use of the word *practices* suggests that they are not acting unselfishly and honestly, that they fit very well into this atmosphere of suspicion and underhandedness. Moreover, certain echoes in their words and in the words addressed to them may be revealing. *"Both* your majesties" might have commanded rather than requested, says Rosencrantz, "we *both* obey," chimes in Guildenstern. The latter goes on to say:

> [We] give up ourselves in the full bent
> To lay our service freely at your feet,
> To be commanded.
>
> (Act II, Sc. 2, 30-32)

This is indeed a strained way of saying that they will honor Claudius' request. "Thanks, Rosencrantz and gentle Guildenstern," says the king; "Thanks, Guildenstern and gentle Rosencrantz," echoes the queen. As one early critic remarked, the parallelism suggests their nullity; it is as if neither were more than half a man.

The return of Cornelius and Voltimand with their report about Fortinbras will have special import much later in the play, but it has some significance here. Among other things, it provides a clear indication of how much time has elapsed since Hamlet saw and listened to the ghost. Also, here is the third reference to the young Norwegian prince who, like Hamlet, has lost a father and who, unlike Hamlet, has promptly taken positive action to avenge his father's death. But Fortinbras, one now learns, has mastered passion; he will obey his royal uncle, rejecting the idea of revenge, and will expend his energy in an attack upon Poland. Fortinbras, it would seem, is emerging as a foil to Hamlet.

Matters relating to foreign relations having been settled, Polonius is ready to demonstrate his wisdom in solving the mystery of Hamlet's behavior. Now he emerges as an utter fool—and as a marvelous comic creation—pompous, smug, and frivolous. The lord chamberlain's repetitions, parallelisms, plays on words—all delivered with supreme confidence in his own ability—result in a full-length picture, perhaps a caricature, of a zany. However exaggerated it may be, Shakespeare prepared his audience for it. Most amusing is the fact that Polonius is his own best critic, as when, after a verbal exercise involving the words *day, night,* and *time,* he concludes:

> Therefore, since brevity is the soul of wit,
> And tediousness the limbs and outward flourishes,
> I will be brief.
>
> (Act II, Sc. 2, 90-92)

And later, despite the queen's admonition that he provide "more matter, with less art," he indulges in another such exercise involving the words *true* and *pity,* and then concludes: "A foolish figure!"

Such broad comedy is welcome as a relief from tragic seriousness; nevertheless, it is functional in relation to the major action. In Hamlet's world, Polonius is accepted as the wise, if not wisest, counselor; and Polonius plays that role with all the art peculiar to his limited character. Respect for age had an important place in Renaissance philosophy, but it did not follow that an individual who had reached, or was close to, old age would be permitted to remain in a public position. It must be assumed that earlier, and with strict reference to ordinary affairs, Polonius had proved satisfactory; if this were not so, surely the competent Claudius would not depend upon him to such an extent.

Hamlet's love letter, which Polonius reads, is a curious composition, what with its stilted prose and bad verse. For once, one must agree with Polonius, who immediately sets himself up as a critic of style: "'beautified' is a vile phrase". It suggests the use of make-up, the "plast'ring art," to use the term both Hamlet and Claudius will employ later.

It is generally agreed that the love letter is part of Hamlet's pretence of madness on the grounds that, unless it were contrived, the scholarly Hamlet could never have written it. Certainly it is consistent with the portrait of a lovesick Hamlet, as described by Ophelia, and what has been said with reference to that is applicable here. It seems reasonable to conclude that Hamlet knew that the letter would fall into the hands of the foolish Polonius. Nevertheless, the first two lines of verse may have some special significance:

> Doubt thou the stars are fire;
> Doubt that the sun doth move;
>
> (Act II, Sc. 5, 116-17)

Doubts relating to the stars and sun in the universe arose in the late Renaissance and represented a challenge to the traditional view of the universe. Some find here evidence that Hamlet, after his crushing discovery of great evil, has lost his faith in traditional values, which includes the belief that woman can be both fair and true. Finally, certain Romantics insist that Hamlet suffers primarily because his love for Ophelia has not been requited. Such emphasis on the love theme, however, seriously reduces the element of conflict involving Hamlet and Claudius, and removes the play itself from the realm of high tragedy.

The king and queen depart with their attendants as soon as they see Hamlet coming. The queen's words, "But look where sadly the poor wretch comes reading," provide useful stage directions, but they do more. They suggest, as do certain other passages in the play, that Gertrude's love and concern for her son are genuine. The ghost, commanding Hamlet to "Leave her to heaven," had called her "a weak vessel"—and so she is, for she willingly became a partner in an incestuous marriage. But her ready response to the attentions of Claudius seems to be the extent of her guilt.

Enter Hamlet, reading. This is the prince who had vowed to "sweep to [his] revenge" without delay, wiping away "all trivial fond records,/All saws of books." Perhaps through such reading and through contemplation, he has gained emotional control. In this episode his antic disposition, manifested in his baiting of Polonius, actually reveals a rational mind. His replies and questions addressed to the lord chamberlain call for rather close attention.

Does Hamlet recognize Polonius? Yes. Polonius is a fishmonger, a name which the lord chamberlain immediately denies. Yet here is Polonius on another fishing expedition using his "bait of falsehood" and, by indirection, seeking to find directions out. Moreover, *fishmonger* was an Elizabethan term for *bawd* (keeper of a whore house)— not an inappropriate word, however vulgar, for a man who has just declared that he would "loose" his daughter on Hamlet.

A disillusioned idealist, the prince seems to be obsessed with the subject of honesty. Among those in authoritative positions, he finds no honesty. Even innocent daughters may be corrupted; even the apparently healthful rays of the sun may lead to the breeding of maggots in a dead dog, "being a good kissing carrion." He does not finish the statement; instead, he suddenly asks Polonius, "Have you a daughter?" Then he provides riddling advice: "Let her not walk i' th' sun. Conception is a blessing, but not as your daughter may conceive."

Page after page has been filled with explication of this brief passage with its plays on the words *sun* and *conception*. Among the interpretations widely accepted is that these lines emphasize (1) Hamlet's awareness of rottenness in the court, and (2) his conviction that Claudius, the new ruler, is the source of that rottenness which threatens to contaminate or destroy all at Elsinore. There remains the possibility that, since Hamlet seems to know that Polonius will "loose" his daughter upon him, Ophelia has become an obsession for Hamlet. The difficulty with this conclusion is that it is exactly the one reached by Polonius. One point is indisputable. Hamlet is overwhelmingly successful in convincing the lord chamberlain that he is "far gone," suffering "much extremity for love."

In warmth, Hamlet's greeting of Rosencrantz and Guildenstern as his "excellent good friends" matches the greeting that he accorded Horatio. It at once gives an insight into the normal mood of Hamlet before his tragedy began and reveals his yearning for honest comradeship. Add to this the fact that again he demonstrates his capacity for a quick change of mood. At first his remarks are spontaneous, good-natured ones; but, not long after the subject of Fortune is introduced, they become serious and revealing—specifically when Rosencrantz remarks that he has no news to report "but that the world's grown honest." Rejecting this conclusion, Hamlet, changing the subject, speaks of Denmark and the world itself as a prison. From this emerges the theme of ambition. Now Hamlet is fully aware of what these two supposed friends are up to. Characteristically, he asks them in the name of friendship to be honest with him; just as characteristically, they seek to evade a direct answer but are practically forced to admit that the king and queen have sent for them.

There follows one of the several especially memorable passages in the play, one in which the prince is again revealed as the disillusioned idealist. Here is a young intellectual who once embraced the Renaissance view of an ordered and moral universe in which man, endowed with reason, was the noblest creature, far above the animal, and near to the angelic realm. According to this concept, inherited from the Middle Ages, man occupies a place on a hierarchical scale midway between the beast and the angel: the first represents absence or rejection of reason; the second, pure reason which is equated with virtue. But Hamlet has learned that mankind has a terrifying capacity to reject reason, to descend to the bestial level: subjects may murder kings, brother may kill brother; wives and mothers may hasten to incestuous beds; boyhood friends may permit themselves to be used as spies, rejecting the sacred principles of friendship. Philosophy offers poor consolation under such conditions. For Hamlet, the world has become "a sterile promontory" and man no more than the "quintessence of dust."

Hamlet's speech (Act II, Sc. 2, 304 ff.), which includes the famous apostrophe to man, has significance in terms of the plot. Hamlet finds it desirable to explain his emotional state to Rosencrantz and Guildenstern, and he does so without revealing its cause. Rosencrantz laughs and makes a humorous remark relating to women, and this provides an easy transition to the next episode in this long scene.

Ultimately the actors will serve the prince in his first positive move against Claudius—reason enough for the announcement of their arrival and for the talk relating to them. But there are other points to be noticed here. "He that plays the king shall be welcome." This is Hamlet's immediate response to the news; it is clearly a reference to Claudius, whom the prince holds to be no more than a player-king, however skilful in acting the part.

Just before the players appear, Polonius enters, confident that only he can inform Hamlet of their arrival. Again he is the target of Hamlet's biting satire. Most of Hamlet's remarks the lord chamberlain either does not hear or, at least, understand. Just as he had set himself up as an authority on word choice, so now he presents himself as one on drama. His catalogue of types of Elizabethan drama provides wonderful comedy, all the more amusing because Polonius remains deadly serious. It also reveals Shakespeare's own familiarity with Elizabethan drama, the classical tragedies of Plautus, the tragedies of Seneca, and (to some extent) dramatic theory. With reference to Polonius, the implication is plain. As his advice to Laertes indicated, he is an educated individual; unfortunately, knowledge does not always lead to wisdom. In Polonius' case, vanity and age have taken their toll. If his methods were not so contemptible, perhaps he would deserve sympathy.

"O Jephthah, judge of Israel, what a treasure hadst thou!" exclaims Hamlet, having adopted the antic pose to the bewilderment of the lord chamberlain. But to paraphrase Polonius' words, there is method in his "madness." Jephthah sacrificed a beloved daughter, however unwillingly; in a sense, Polonius is sacrificing his daughter.

Hamlet then greets the players, once more demonstrating a rapid change in mood. His warmth and genuine pleasure are apparent. Here, then, is another glimpse of Hamlet's mood prior to his discovery of appalling evil. This Wittenberg student, devoted to his studies, nevertheless enjoyed the theater just as he treasured companionship. His witty, good-natured remarks to the bearded player and to the youth who had played women's roles suggest a Hamlet who is anything but a dreamer.

Having made the arrangements for the performance of *The Murder of Gonzago* with the insertion of lines to be provided by him, Hamlet is left alone; again he soliloquizes at length. The prince now emerges as his own severest critic, denouncing himself as "a dull and muddy-mettled [irresolute] rascal," a dreamer "unpregnant of [unstirred by] my cause." But, rather curiously, it is the actor's description of Hecuba's display of sorrow for the death of Priam that Hamlet most wanted to hear and which leads him to chastise himself, insisting that he has greater "motive and the cue for passion." Passionate expression of grief is not positive action; indeed, it inhibits action. One wonders why the prince did not dwell upon Pyrrhus' act of vengeance which seems to have unmistakable applicability to Hamlet. Pyrrhus, enraged by the violent death of his father, Achilles, is determined to execute vengeance on King Priam, father of Achilles' slayer. Pyrrhus did delay, but only momentarily:

> For, lo! his sword,
> Which was declining on the milky head
> Of reverend Priam, seem'd i' th' air to stick.
> So as a painted tyrant Pyrrhus stood
> And like a neutral to his will and matter
> Did nothing.

> (Act II, Sc. 2, 465-70)

Hamlet unmistakably sees himself as "a neutral to his will and matter." In the lines spoken by the player, Pyrrhus promptly emerges as the perfect avenger, the very prototype of the king-killer:

And never did the Cyclops' hammers fall
On Mars' armor forged for proof eterne,
With less remorse than Pyrrhus' bleeding sword
Now falls on Priam.

                              (Act II, Sc. 2, 477-80)

A whole school of critics, beginning with the Romantics, have taken Hamlet's self-criticism as the essential truth: he is the hopeless dreamer; he cannot bring himself to act positively until it is too late to prevent his own downfall. But is one to assume that Hamlet, scholar and son of a father idolized for his superior virtues, would identify himself with the blood-smeared Pyrrhus who made "malicious sport/In mincing with his sword [Priam's] limbs?" If the Greek warrior is held to be the model of the dutiful son avenging his father's death, little wonder that Hamlet said, after hearing the ghost's accusation, "O cursed spite,/That ever I was born to set it right." Yet so intense are his feelings at this point that Hamlet denounces himself as a coward, apparently for not having acted as promptly as Pyrrhus did. Hamlet reaches the climax of passion as he denounces Claudius and cries out for vengeance:

                              Bloody, bawdy villain!
Remorseless, treacherous, lecherous, kindless
villain!
O, vengeance!

                              (Act II, Sc. 2, 565-67)

But Hamlet masters his fury; he is aware that he has permitted passion, not reason, to dominate him. It is now that he reveals his plan to "catch the conscience of the king"—unmistakably to establish Claudius' guilt.

Little wonder that *Hamlet* has been referred to sometimes as "The Mystery of Hamlet." In the last scene of Act I, Hamlet vowed to sweep to his revenge; weeks have passed and he has not made even an attempt. Many have argued that the wary Claudius, well-protected by his palace guard, has not given the prince a chance to attack him. But there is another complication. After rejoining Marcellus and Horatio, Hamlet declared, "It is an honest ghost, that let me tell you." Now, at the end of Act II, he has genuine doubts regarding the nature of the ghost and feels compelled to confirm its testimony. So far, only when he was in a state of great excitement marked by "wild and whirling words" has Hamlet had no doubts about the ghost. Although he becomes quite excited emotionally at the climax of his soliloquy, he controls himself and he immediately plans to verify the ghost's accusation. The conclusion to be drawn is that when Hamlet is in control of his passion, he recognizes, as Horatio did, that the ghost may represent evil.

Some critics insist that this entire scene serves first of all to emphasize Hamlet's inability to act positively. Does not the prince refer to his "weakness" and his "melancholy?" And was it not the lines dealing with Hecuba's grief which he was most anxious to hear? Certain distinguished Shakespeareans find Hamlet to be a victim of passion—the passion of excessive grief which was known as melancholy adust. Whether or not one agrees that Hamlet delays fatally because he is the victim of the destructive passion of melancholy, the subject deserves attention. Certainly it would be a mistake to ignore the many textual references, direct and indirect, to melancholy. For the immediate purpose, it must suffice to state that when Hamlet speaks of the world as a prison, when he declares that he has "foregone all custom of exercise" and that for him the earth seems to be "a sterile promontory" and the air "a foul and pestilent congregation of vapours," when he tells Rosencrantz and Guildenstern that he is "but mad north-north-west," and that he knows "a hawk from a handsaw" when "the wind is southerly," the ideas and words derive from prevailing Renaissance theories on melancholy. According to the theorists, the melancholy individual was prone to dwelling at inordinate length upon his difficulties, real or imagined; but, so far from remaining lethargic, he often would become hysterical and would act impulsively. It must be admitted that much of this could be considered applicable to Hamlet. But, of course, one's sympathies remain with him. He indeed has "great cause"—the moral "falling off" of a mother; the death of a beloved father and king; the survival and elevation to kingship of a man who, however clever, is obviously inferior to the late King Hamlet.

It is a completely controlled, rational Hamlet who speaks the lines at the very end of this long, complex scene:

> I'll have grounds
> More relative than this. The play's the thing
> Wherein I'll catch the conscience of the king.
>
> (Act II, Sc. 2, 589-91)

Some stage Hamlets—the late John Barrymore, for example—rendered these lines hysterically; those who grasped the character and situation accurately—Sir John Gielgud, for example—spoke them with vigor and determination, and without raving.

ACT III • SCENE 1

Summary
Rosencrantz and Guildenstern report to the king and queen that Hamlet admits feeling "distracted" but will not tell them the cause and

keeps himself aloof "with a crafty madness." In reply to Gertrude's question, they report that Hamlet received them graciously and seemed pleased to hear of the players' arrival. Polonius adds that the prince wants the king and queen to witness the performance of a play. Claudius expresses his pleasure at hearing that Hamlet shows such an interest and agrees to attend the performance. He then instructs Rosencrantz and Guildenstern to encourage Hamlet's new interest. The two depart.

At the king's request, Gertrude leaves. Now Polonius' plan to have Ophelia meet Hamlet while the king and the lord chamberlain secretly observe and listen can be put into effect. Polonius instructs his daughter: Ophelia is to appear to be reading a book of devotions so that the prince will not suspect her purpose. In an aside, Claudius reveals the extent to which Polonius' words lash his conscience. Counselor and king withdraw just before Hamlet enters.

For the third time in the play, Hamlet soliloquizes. He now ponders the question of "To be, or not to be" when one is faced with great difficulties and tribulations. At the sight of Ophelia, he is aroused from contemplation. Assuming that she is indeed reading a book of devotions, he urges her to pray for him.

When Ophelia says that she has certain gifts which she has received from him and now wishes to return, he declares that he has given her nothing. To her bewilderment, he proceeds to question her honesty and denies that he ever loved her, whatever he may have said in the past. All men, Hamlet declares, are "arrant knaves;" none should be believed. Therefore, he concludes, she should seek haven in a nunnery. Quite abruptly the prince asks Ophelia where her father is. She replies that he is at home. Again he returns to the general subject of love, declaring that, should she ever marry, she will "not escape calumny." And again he gives her bitter advice: "Get thee to a nunnery, go." Left to herself, Ophelia expresses her profound sorrow at witnessing what she is convinced is the overthrow of a noble mind.

Promptly, the king and Polonius join Ophelia. Claudius now is convinced that love is not the cause of Hamlet's affliction; rather, that it is "something in his soul/O'er which his melancholy sits on brood." No less convinced that Hamlet's behavior constitutes a great threat to him, the king tells Polonius that he has suddenly decided to have Hamlet conducted to England, whose ruler owes tribute to Denmark. Polonius is still convinced that the prince suffers from love-madness, but he approves Claudius' decision. He then tells his daughter that she need not say anything since the king and he heard all. The lord chamberlain urges that one more attempt be made to ferret out Hamlet's secret: let the queen talk with her son severely on the subject of his melancholy while Polonius listens from a place of concealment; then, if Hamlet's secret is not exposed, let Claudius send the prince to England or confine him elsewhere. "It shall be so," says the king. "Madness in great ones must not unwatch'd go."

Commentary

It is an increasingly fearful Claudius who appears in this first scene of Act III, although he remains in control of himself. As the conflict between him and Hamlet intensifies, he demonstrates his decisiveness, his capacity for immediate action. His control is especially obvious in his care to keep up the appearance of being unselfishly concerned about his nephew's well-being and in the apparent graciousness with which he agrees promptly to honor Hamlet's request that he and the queen witness the performance of the play. But the intensity of his concern makes it clear that he recognizes Hamlet's so-called "turbulent . . . lunacy" as a dangerous threat to himself.

Claudius' aside explicitly reveals the mind of a man tormented by guilt. In his aside, Claudius applies the words to himself: "How smart a lash that speech doth give my conscience!" He compares his "painted word"—what he says publicly—to the "harlot's cheek, beautied with plast'ring art." Illicit sex or lust, here represented by the harlot, symbolizes pervading evil and man's descent to the level of beasts. "O heavy burden!" the king concludes. He has emerged as a human being, however sinful.

Needless to say, Claudius remains the powerful adversary. He is Machiavellian not only in his ability to lie and in his use of underhanded methods, but also in his capacity for prompt action. Rosencrantz and Guildenstern are directed to renew their efforts and Polonius will be given another chance to verify his judgment. But the king stands ready to send Hamlet away—not back to Wittenberg, but to England, where he can be 'taken care of.'

Both Polonius and Gertrude remain in character. The lord chamberlain is the author of what Claudius chooses to call "lawful espials;" it is he who coaches his daughter on how to play her ignoble part; it is he who remains vainly confident that only he is qualified to counsel the king. If Polonius acknowledges blame for using under-handed methods, he seems to do so only in vanity, welcoming this chance to display himself as a man of wisdom.

As before, Gertrude shows proper motherly concern for an ailing son. In this connection, it will be noted that she is the one who asks if Rosencrantz and Guildenstern have tried to interest Hamlet in some amusement or other. But also, as before, the queen accepts uncritically whatever Claudius says and willingly gives in to his wishes. She is the dutiful wife, to be sure—but in a marriage that is incestuous.

The "To be, or not to be" soliloquy is surely one of the great dramatic monologues in world literature; it is as well known as any passage in Shakespeare, and a favorite selection for memorization. The prince's meditation transcends the personal. Much of what he says is applicable to all mankind, especially when he provides a generalized list of human miseries:

For, who would bear the whips and scorns of time,
Th' oppressor's wrong, the proud man's contumely
The pangs of despis'd love, the law's delay,
The insolence of office, and the spurns
That patient merit of th' unworthy takes, . . .

(Act III, Sc. 1, 70-74)

The entire speech has been called the "central soliloquy" in the play, coming as it does at the midpoint of the entire action. It poses many critical problems. In view of the often widely varying interpretations of this soliloquy, it would be naïve to ignore the difficulties of interpretation.

In the first place, the soliloquy comes as something of a surprise after the conclusion of Act II, which exhibited Hamlet as rational and determined, intent upon carrying out a positive action that, he was sure, would resolve all doubts relating to Claudius. Now he seems to have reverted to the mood of the first soliloquy—the mood of the prince who would welcome death, crushed as he was primarily by his mother's marriage to her brother-in-law. There are lines which may support any one of the major interpretations of the play. The Romantics, who see Hamlet as the dreamer, find support when the prince says:

And thus the native hue of resolution
Is sicklied o'er with the pale cast of thought,
And enterprises of great pitch and moment
With this regard their currents turn awry
And lose the name of action.

(Act III, Sc. 1, 84-88)

Those who are convinced that the tragic hero procrastinates because he is suffering from excessive grief find in the soliloquy one of those violent changes of mood typical of the extreme melancholic individual, although the subsequent episode involving Ophelia provides a better example. And then there is that considerable group who finds in this soliloquy evidence of Hamlet's moral principles which makes it impossible for him to abandon the resources of God-given reason and sweep to his revenge in the manner of Pyrrhus. In his restraint they find an intellectual skepticism and honesty with himself that are commendable. For all three groups of theorists, Hamlet's eloquent speech explains his expression of despair at the end of Act I, Scene 5:

The time is out of joint;—O cursed spite,
That ever I was born to set it right.

"To be, or not to be: that is the question." So Hamlet begins his contemplations. In view of his words shortly thereafter, the assumption is usually made that he is asking whether one should choose to live or to die. But immediately after posing the question, the prince defines two possible courses, neither one of which involves death and certainly not suicide. First, he asks if passive acceptance of "outrageous fortune" is not the nobler course to follow. According to the dedicated Stoic, pagan and Christian, the final aim of moral action is to destroy passion since no action can be virtuous unless it proceeds from a healthy and upright will. The second course involves positive action— taking "arms against a sea of troubles." The young prince next considers a third possible solution to his problem—suicide. Hamlet states, in effect, that oblivion may be preferable—but only if death brings oblivion:

> To die, to sleep—
> To sleep—Perchance to dream: ay, there's the
> rub
> For in that sleep of death what dreams may come,
> When we have shuffled off this mortal coil,
> Must give us pause.
>
> (Act III, Sc. 1, 64-68)

The reason for this fear of death (if that is what it is) is made more explicit in three memorable lines:

> But that the dread of something after death,
> The undiscovered country from whose bourn
> No traveller returns, puzzles the will, . . .
>
> (Act III, Sc. 1, 78-80)

How are these lines to be interpreted? Does Hamlet reject the possibility that the ghost was the spirit of his father? Earlier in the play he spoke of his soul as immortal. Why now should it be that the thought of death "puzzles the will?" The ghost described its condition of afterlife, not as an "undiscover'd country" but as the Catholic purgatory necessary for the soul's purification before translation to heaven. Has Hamlet now embraced the Elizabethan Protestant belief, stated and amplified in sermon and devotional literature that, once separated from the body, the soul cannot return to this world? Perhaps Shakespeare has simply made poetic use of what had become a popular tradition by the time he wrote *Hamlet*. There may be another explanation; Shakespeare may have had in mind the difference between the return from the grave of an individual like Lazarus in flesh and blood, in contrast to the return of the spirit, or soul. But one thing is clear. Hamlet has not departed from Christianity; there is no evidence that he doubts the existence of heaven and hell, both of which prompt him to his revenge, or so he has said.

But the prince has been restrained by doubts relating to the nature of the ghost that would have him execute prompt revenge on Claudius but have him leave Gertrude "to heaven." There are two other possible reasons for Hamlet's delay. The players have just arrived at Elsinore, and only now does Hamlet have an opportunity to force Claudius into a position where the guilt acknowledged in his private thoughts may be exposed publicly. There is also the possibility that he is held back by his awareness of his intense personal hatred of his uncle-king. Schooled in idealistic philosophy and religious thought, he may believe that his motive for action is not a pure one—that the personal element contaminates that of public justice. If any or all of this is true, then the soliloquy is not to be interpreted as just another instance of morbid contemplation peculiar to a philosophical dreamer or to an individual suffering from the passion of excessive grief.

The episode which follows provides a shocking change of mood and shows a Hamlet cruel in his treatment of Ophelia. Shakespeare prepared his audience for this episode which relates back to the one in Act II, Scene 2, where Hamlet baited Polonius with riddling words: "Let her [your daughter] not walk i' th' sun. Conception is a blessing, but not as your daughter may conceive. Friend, look to't." Polonius has not looked to it; in the king's service, he has "loosed" Ophelia upon Hamlet. As in the earlier episode, the prince introduces the theme of honesty—an obsession with him, be it with reference to his own grief ("Seems, madam! Nay, it is; I know not 'seems.'"), the nature of the ghost, the behavior of one-time friends, or the moral character of women. In view of all this, it is difficult to avoid the conclusion that Hamlet, like members of the audience, is fully aware of what is happening: Ophelia is being used just as Rosencrantz and Guildenstern were used; the king and Polonius are spying on him even now. Hamlet, it would appear, is only too aware that Ophelia represents "innocent love" corrupted—coming to him not of her own will but as a spy. And the ultimate source of the corruption is King Claudius, who rules in a world where women prove "frail" and few men can be believed.

Hamlet's mood is exactly that which dominated him when he said to Rosencrantz and Guildenstern, "Man delights not me,—no, nor woman neither, though by your smiling you seem to say so." No individual can escape contamination in the world as Hamlet now finds it. Not without logic, then, the disillusioned prince declares that he had never given Ophelia tokens of love and that he was never honest with her:

You should not have believed me, for virtue cannot
so innoculate our old stock but we shall relish of it.

I loved you not.

(Act III, Sc. 1, 117-19)

In other words, since the Fall of Adam and Eve, all are sinners; none can escape corruption. Hamlet accuses himself of pride, vengefulness, selfish ambition—indeed of more offenses than he is able to think of: "We are arrant knaves all; believe none of us." These words are heard by Ophelia and overheard by Claudius and Polonius; but Hamlet really speaks to and for Everyman.

What then can Ophelia do? Hamlet tells her: "Go thy ways to a nunnery." That he is fully aware that Ophelia has been and remains chaste, that she is the victim of a father incapable of honest methods, is shown in Hamlet's warning:

> If thou dost marry, I'll give thee this plague for thy dowry: be thou as chaste as ice, as pure as snow, thou shalt not escape calumny. Get thee to a nunnery.

(Act III, Sc. 1, 137-39)

Surely these lines would have little significance if Ophelia were un-chaste and if Hamlet were not aware of how she had been "loosed" upon him.

There is a second level of meaning here, one which is consistent with Hamlet's bitter statement that time has proven feminine beauty and honesty to be incompatible. In the present scene, he says that women make monsters of the men they marry, and, like the harlots of whom the conscience-stricken Claudius spoke in his aside, their cheeks are "beautied with plast'ring art" and they seek to excuse their immorality as ignorance. After this devastating pronouncement, Hamlet repeats the order: "To a nunnery, go." In the slang of the militantly Protestant Elizabethan England, the term *nunnery* also meant "brothel." No member of Shakespeare's sixteenth- and seventeenth-century audience was likely to miss this second level of meaning.

Left to herself, Ophelia speaks lines which at once reveal the genuineness of her lost love and provide a full-length portrait of Hamlet before his tragedy began. It is the picture of the completely accomplished Renaissance man:

> O, what a noble mind is here o'erthrown!
> The courtier's, soldier's, scholar's, eye, tongue, sword,
> Th' expectancy and rose of the fair state,
> The glass of fashion and the mould of form,
> Th' observ'd of all observers, quite, quite down!

(Act III, Sc. 1, 150-54)

She is convinced that Hamlet is insane. He is not, however emotionally disturbed he may be. Nevertheless, it is possible that she expresses a basic truth—or so some respected critics believe. Perhaps Hamlet's suffering has resulted in such extreme disillusionment and melancholy that a once-noble mind has been overthrown in the sense that he has become passion's slave. Certainly this interpretation is not to be ignored.

Emerging with Polonius from the hiding place, Claudius rejects the theory that his nephew suffers from love-madness, but, like his lord chamberlain, he is aware of an apparent method in the prince's alleged madness. In a state of uncertainty, he will allow Polonius another chance to force Hamlet into revealing the cause of his strange behavior. But if that fails, the king will have Hamlet sent to England. It is to be noted that Claudius continues to present the public image of a man who is unselfishly concerned and especially of one dedicated to the welfare of the state.

ACT III • SCENE 2

Summary

Hamlet instructs the players in how to deliver the lines of *The Murder of Gonzago* and discusses the art of acting in general, urging them to avoid unnatural extremes in the imitation of an action. Polonius enters with Rosencrantz and Guildenstern; he announces that the king and the queen are ready to "hear" the play.

While members of the court assemble, Hamlet praises Horatio for his steady temperament and then gives him the details relating to *The Murder of Gonzago*. He asks Horatio to keep close watch on the king, just as he himself will do, and to note the king's reaction to one speech in particular. If Claudius does not reveal guilt at that point, the prince continues, both have seen "a damned ghost," not the honest spirit of the late King Hamlet. The faithful Horatio assures the prince that he will follow the instructions carefully.

The court group enters the hall. Claudius greets his nephew and receives a baffling reply. There follows a brief exchange between Hamlet and Polonius. When his mother invites him to sit beside her, Hamlet declines, lying down at Ophelia's feet.

The play itself is preceded by a dumb-show or pantomime, depicting a king and queen deeply in love with each other. When the king falls asleep on a bed of flowers, the queen departs. A man enters, removes the king's crown and kisses it, pours poison into the king's ear, and leaves. The queen returns, finds her husband dead, and expresses grief. The murderer returns and, after the king's body has been carried away, woos the queen. At first she resists his attentions, but soon accepts his love.

In answer to Ophelia's question, Hamlet assures her that the actor who enters to speak the lines of the prologue will "tell all"—that is, explain the significance of the action. When the four lines of the prologue are recited, Ophelia remarks that it is brief. "As woman's love," Hamlet replies. The performance of the play then commences.

The action in *The Murder of Gonzago* is the same as that depicted in the dumb-show up to the point where the murderer, identified as one Lucianus, nephew to the king, pours the poison in the king's ear. The queen is emphatic in her declaration never to remarry should she become a widow. In the words of the player-king, spoken as he is about to "beguile/The tedious day with sleep," "'Tis deeply sworn."

The brief interlude gives Hamlet the opportunity to ask Gertrude how she likes the play. "The lady doth protest too much," she replies. Claudius then asks Hamlet if he is familiar with the dramatic story and if it is in any way an offense. The prince replies: "No, no, they do but jest, poison in jest." Again in reply to a question by Claudius, he explains that the play is called "The Mouse-trap." The prince's words to Ophelia especially reveal his state of excitement. He calls upon the actor playing the role of the murderer to stop grimacing and begin to speak his lines. All along he has been, as Ophelia says, "a good chorus." When the murderer pours the poison into the player-king's ear, he assures the audience that this is the dramatization of an actual murder and that they will see how the murderer "gets the love of Gonzago's wife."

Alarmed, Claudius rises. Polonius calls for an end of the play. The king cries out: "Give me some light. Away!" All but Hamlet and Horatio leave the hall. It is a triumphant prince who, after indulging in ironic banter with Horatio, declares that he will "take the ghost's word for a thousand pound." Horatio agrees that the king reacted like a guilty man.

Rosencrantz and Guildenstern return to inform Hamlet that the king is greatly disturbed and that the queen wishes to speak with her son privately. Hamlet's ironic remarks reveal his contempt for these so-called friends who will not be forthright with him and presume to think that they can "pluck out the heart of [his] mystery." Polonius enters with the same message for Hamlet: the queen wishes to speak with him. Again the prince adopts the antic style, voicing absurd irrelevancies before he informs the lord chamberlain that he will honor his mother's request. He is then left to himself.

Now Hamlet's words, spoken in soliloquy, reveal a bloodthirsty mood. But he counsels himself not to inflict physical harm upon his mother, to whose chamber he will now go: "Let me be cruel, not unnatural," he says.

Commentary

Hamlet's advice to the players, which takes up some fifty lines, seems on the surface to be interesting primarily not for what it contributes to *Hamlet* but for what one learns about Shakespeare, the professional actor and playwright concerned that actors do justice to his script. Scholars have pointed out that a rival company of actors was noted for 'splitting the ears of the groundlings', those less affluent members of the audience who stood in the pit of the theater, serving those who confused pompous speech with eloquence and realism. That there is a personal element here seems likely, especially when Hamlet says, "And let those that play your clowns speak no more than is set down for them," advice hardly applicable to actors performing *The Murder of Gonzago*.

This episode also provides a release of tension after the disturbing nunnery scene. And again it provides evidence of Hamlet's variety of character and normal interests. He is shown to have been a young man who enjoyed the theater and as one whose critical judgment has been highly developed. If nothing else, this tends to refute the theory that the prince was the complete introvert, just as it adds somewhat to his intellectual stature.

Hamlet's chief concern in this episode is that *The Murder of Gonzago* be so performed that it will be a convincing imitation of life itself and, in this sense, will hold "the mirror up to nature." Only then can he be sure that it will provide the test of Claudius' conscience. If an unskilful player oversteps "the modesty of nature," presenting a "whirlwind of passion" which "out-herods Herod" (a character in the mystery plays notorious for pomp), the performance cannot possibly impress the courtly audience as worthy of serious consideration.

But there is more here. At another level, Hamlet is providing a commentary on mankind in general and making a plea for the use of God-given reason and a concern for truth as opposed to appearance. In a word, let man justify his supposed status as a "wondrous work" and the "paragon of animals." When the prince speaks of holding the mirror up to nature, one inevitably recalls Ophelia's tribute to a Hamlet who had been the "glass of fashion and the mould of form." Moreover, this episode looks forward to Hamlet's praise of Horatio as one who is not passion's slave.

Hamlet's praise of Horatio has been accepted by a great many commentators as the passage which establishes Horatio as the norm character in relation to the tragic hero—that is, as the individual in the play who possesses the very qualities which Hamlet should have if he is to avoid tragic downfall. The young man whom the prince so much admires is depicted as the true Stoic, one who accepts "Fortune's buffets" (strokes of ill fortune) with good grace because he maintains proper balance between "blood and judgment"—that is, between emotion and reason—and thus is not "passion's slave." One can understand why many believe this passage provides a key to the interpretation of *Hamlet*. Certainly the commoner Horatio, admirable as he is, has never been put to a test comparable to that which Hamlet faces: tragic heroes must be tested and the test must be a great one.

Hamlet requests Horatio to watch the king closely to see if

Claudius' "occulted [hidden] guilt/Do not itself unkennel in one speech." It is of some interest to know that the prince now has *his* spy. At Elsinore, where "seeming" and the use of indirections are commonplace, he will fight fire with fire. Ophelia has been "loosed" upon him; now he will have Horatio help in "unkenneling" Claudius' secret.

As all prepare to see the play, Hamlet's state of high excitement comes through. "I must be idle," he says to Horatio, and this is a cue that he will adopt the antic pose again. This pose gives him the opportunity to make remarks to the king, to Polonius, and to Ophelia which may be interpreted as evidence of mental instability and, at the same time, serve to perplex a vitally concerned listener like Claudius.

For his purpose, Hamlet must find a place where he can closely watch Claudius. But in his reply to Gertrude's invitation that he sit next to her, he is able to contribute to Polonius' theory; that is, he is mad for the love of Ophelia. The bawdy remarks he makes to that young lady carry forward the theme of honesty in women. "You are merry, my lord," says Ophelia. Hamlet's reply reveals his state of tension and his disillusionment: "O God, your only jig-maker." His lines which follow are packed with bitterness, and his ironic reference to the length of man's memory may be an indictment not only of Gertrude but also of himself: "Remember me," the ghost had stated repeatedly. Hamlet, who had then declared that he would sweep to his revenge without delay, is reminded in this episode that four months have elapsed since his father's death.

Especially in pre-Shakespearean drama, the dumb-show was used to indicate action which was not presented in the play proper or to symbolize what was to be presented. The dumb-show here poses certain problems. It is certainly not one of those "inexplicable dumb-shows" Hamlet had criticized earlier. It includes most of the circumstances of the murder as told by the ghost, although it includes nothing suggesting that Gertrude was unfaithful to King Hamlet when he was alive or that she was involved in the murder. Why did Shakespeare include this dumb-show? Why is not Claudius startled and aroused by it? These have been lingering questions among Shakespearean critics.

The prince's reaction to having caught the conscience of the King in the Mouse-trap is not one of horror but of elation—understandably because, despite his expression of doubt, he now has absolute proof of Claudius' guilt. Perhaps he is relieved especially because he can act as one executing public justice, not just as a son carrying out blood revenge in accordance with an old, barbaric code. The difficulty, however, is that nowhere in the play does Hamlet explicitly question the propriety of revenge. The ghost spoke truly: Claudius is guilty of fratricide and regicide. But is Hamlet to emerge as minister (one righteously carrying out God's vengeance upon a sinner) or as scourge (one whose sinful act of taking vengeance into his own hands God permits for His own purpose, but who ultimately will face God's punishment). Again, it should be noted, Hamlet's prime concern has been to establish Claudius' guilt, not the "honesty" of the ghost. All this deserves notice if one is to do justice to the play and to understand why it has been subject to apparently endless discussion. But this is not to deny that readers and audiences have not the slightest doubt that Hamlet, prince of Denmark, should slay Claudius and remove the source of all rottenness in the state.

Hamlet's mood of excitement and elation is sustained in the first part of his dialogue with Rosencrantz and Guildenstern, one of whom informs him that the king is "In his retirement marvellous distemper'd" "With drink, sir?" asks Hamlet, and one is reminded of his "dram of evil" speech, voiced when he waited for the appearance of the ghost. In this current display of the antic disposition, his discourse, wild though it sounds to the king's spies, shows method and basic rationality. This becomes apparent when, after stating that he will obey his mother's request, Hamlet asks, "Have you any further trade with us?"—using the plural form of the pronoun and thus presenting himself to them not as a former schoolfellow and as a friend, but as the prince of Denmark. His use of irony is quite bitter and penetrating when he assures Rosencrantz and Guildenstern "by these pickers and stealers" that he still loves them. In an earlier scene, when they first sought him out, Hamlet had spoken of handshaking as the "appurtenance of welcome" employed as a matter of fashion and ceremony; his reference here to hands and fingers as "pickers and stealers" is far more devastating. Apparently Hamlet enjoys misleading these two.

When one of the players reenters with a recorder (an old type of flute), Hamlet, deadly serious, finds an even more devastating way of showing his contempt for Guildenstern. His longer speech at this point has wider application. Guildenstern states that he lacks the skill to play a recorder; yet he is presumptuous enough to think that he can "play" upon Hamlet, as the latter makes abundantly clear:

> 'Sblood,
> do you think I am easier to be play'd on than a pipe? Call me
> what instrument you will, though you can fret me, you
> cannot play upon me.
>
> (Act III, Sc. 2, 355-57)

In his praise of his true friend Horatio, Hamlet had lauded those who "are not a pipe for fortune's finger/To sound what stop she please." Now, having forced Claudius to reveal his guilt, perhaps Hamlet is announcing his right to be numbered as one of those.

Polonius, that easy target for Hamlet's barbs, enters. Once more he is the bearer of stale news, and once more this old counselor renders

61

himself ridiculous. He does, however, get an answer from the prince; Hamlet will come to his mother.

So far in this scene, Hamlet has shown first the mood of the decisive, composed intellectual in his advice to the players; next, the mood of the generous-minded and idealistic friend in his warm praise of Horatio; then the mood of satirical gaiety in his words to the king, Polonius, and Ophelia; and last, the mood of contempt and aloofness in his words to Rosencrantz and Guildenstern. Now, speaking in soliloquy at the end of this climactic scene, he provides a prime example of a shocking shift in emotion. This is not the Hamlet who exclaimed "O cursed spite,/That ever I was born to set it right!"—the Hamlet who drew back at the thought of being called upon to execute vengeance. Rather it is the Hamlet who, immediately after hearing the ghost's story, condemned Gertrude ("O most pernicious woman!") and Claudius ("O villain, villain, smiling, damned villain!"). It is the Hamlet who, in his second soliloquy, after having called himself "a rogue and peasant slave," cried out:

> Bloody, bawdy villain!
> Remorseless, treacherous, lecherous, kindless villain!
> O, vengeance!
>
> (Act II, Sc. 2, 565-67)

If anything, his words here are even more highly charged, what with the reference to yawning churchyards (open graves), hell's contagion, and (the very language of a Black Mass) drinking hot blood. These are words one would expect to hear not from the gifted hero of a high tragedy but rather from the protagonist in a melodramatic revenge play; they are not those of a tragic hero intent upon executing public justice, but of an individual determined to carry out blood revenge come what may. Yet Shakespeare has provided motivation, and Hamlet's emotional stress is understandable.

But, characteristically, Hamlet checks himself: "Soft! now to my mother./O heart, lose not thy nature." That his mother's sin remains a great part of his tragedy is re-emphasized. Hamlet prays that he will not follow the example of the matricidal Nero. He will "be cruel, not unnatural"; he will "speak daggers to her, but use none."

ACT III • SCENE 3

Summary

The king informs Rosencrantz and Guildenstern that, since it is unsafe to let Hamlet's "madness range," they are commissioned to conduct the prince to England as soon as possible. Guildenstern and Rosencrantz express their dedication to the service of the king and their conviction that the welfare of the state depends upon his health and safety. They assure the king that they will waste no time in carrying out his instructions.

Polonius enters and reports that Hamlet is going to his mother's chamber and that he himself will hide behind the arras (wall hanging of tapestry) to hear what is said. Claudius thanks him, and the lord chamberlain departs.

Alone, a conscience-stricken Claudius reveals his thoughts. He identifies himself with Cain, the first murderer and the first man to commit fratricide, and asks himself whether or not, in view of the magnitude of his crime, he can hope for divine mercy. He answers his own question: Christian mercy is denied to no one who repents. But he knows full well that penance is more than the expression of regret; restitution is also necessary. Since he will not give up either the crown or his dead brother's wife, the effects of prayer are denied him. In despair and torment he cries out: "Help, angels! Make assay!" and he expresses the fervent hope that "All may be well" as he kneels in an attempt to pray.

Hamlet enters with drawn sword but restrains himself from slaying Claudius because his father was killed before he could be forgiven for his sins. Hamlet is determined that Claudius will die in a state of sin: hell, not heaven or even purgatory, must be his destination. The prince leaves for his mother's chamber. The king rises, aware that his words "fly up" but that his "thoughts remain below."

Commentary

Claudius' soliloquy provides a second and far more detailed self-acknowledgment of guilt. Villain though he is, Claudius (like Macbeth and in contrast to such a dedicated sinner as Richard III) possesses a conscience, one which hardly makes him cowardly but rather makes him an erring human being, not an inhuman monster. Claudius clearly is not a born villain; however much he has sought to conceal his real self from others, he does not seek to avoid moral and religious truth. He is well-schooled in Christian doctrine, and is fully aware that, so long as he holds on to what he has gained through acts of mortal sin, he cannot rid his soul of guilt. At this particular moment in the action, it is possible to feel some pity for this tormented man despite his crimes.

The Hamlet whose thoughts are revealed when he comes upon Claudius kneeling in an attempt to pray has startled and offended one commentator after another over the years. Hamlet's words, some insist, shock any humane person. It is undeniable that personal hatred, not just the concern for executing justice, motivates the prince in this speech. He would see Claudius eternally damned, not just deprived of mortality. But if it is possible to find sympathy for Claudius the tormented sinner, it is possible to understand Hamlet's inability to shake off the personal anger against the man who killed his father and married his mother.

Among the Romantics, all this is held to be another, crucial example of Hamlet's indecision. It is argued that he is indulging in self-deception, grasping at another excuse for delay. Romantics (and other critics, for that matter) long since have found here the turning-point in the play. Indeed, had Hamlet killed Claudius in this scene, all other violent deaths, especially that of the tragic hero, would not have occurred. In reply, one may point out the obvious: the play would end prematurely and it would be a very unsatisfactory melodrama which ends abruptly after introducing profound questions and complexities of character. More important is this question: who would like to have a Hamlet who, in a bloodthirsty mood, swept to his revenge, slaughtering the kneeling King? Despite all that one has learned about him up to this point in the action, Hamlet could not win sympathy; such a bloody act would lead to the conclusion that indeed a noble mind had been overthrown.

A last point may be made. Ironically, Hamlet is restrained by the belief that Claudius is making a "good" confession and thus escaping damnation. But Claudius' soliloquy reveals that he is unable to do so.

ACT III • SCENE 4

Summary

Polonius has preceded Hamlet to the queen's chamber and now instructs her to be firm with her son. He hides behind the arras just before the prince enters.

Gertrude begins to reprove her son firmly, but his replies and his insistence that she sit down and listen to him so frighten her that she calls out for help. From behind the arras, Polonius echoes her cry. Promptly Hamlet draws his sword, runs it through the arras, and kills the lord chamberlain. "Is it the king?" he asks his mother. But Gertrude can only exclaim upon the monstrosity of the deed. Fiercely Hamlet replies: "Almost as bad, good mother,/As kill a king, and marry with his brother." Only then does he lift up the arras and reveal the dead Polonius, whom he describes as a fool.

The prince then begins to reprimand Gertrude. He shows her contrasting portraits, one of King Hamlet, whom he praises, the other of Claudius, whom he condemns. How, he asks, could she have given herself to Claudius? Hamlet, in effect, answers his own question, accusing his mother of lustfulness. The tormented Gertrude begs him to speak no more.

Suddenly the ghost appears—but only to Hamlet, who is sure that it comes to fault him for his delay. Solemnly the ghost says that it comes "to whet [Hamlet's] almost blunted purpose." But immediately it expresses concern for Gertrude, who is convinced that her son has lost his mind. At its urging, Hamlet speaks gently to his mother, but becomes highly excited in his effort to convince her of the presence of King Hamlet's spirit. The ghost departs.

When Gertrude expresses her conviction that her son is the victim of a hallucination, Hamlet replies that it is not madness that he has spoken and pleads with her to acknowledge her guilt, confessing herself to heaven. At least, he says, let her "assume a virtue," or take the first step toward virtue by avoiding Claudius' bed. Now in a calmer mood, the prince points to the body of Polonius and voices his regret for the death of the lord chamberlain. He bids his mother goodnight and adds that he must be cruel only to be kind. But when she asks what she must do, his reply is bitterly ironic: let her return to Claudius; let her report that he is "mad in craft." Is that not the duty of a loving queen? Gertrude vows that she will not breathe a word of what her son has said to her.

Hamlet tells his mother that he is being sent to England, accompanied by his two schoolfellows whom he completely distrusts. Convinced that they function as agents for his destruction, he will turn the tables on them. In this mood of violent determination, the prince coldly states that he will remove Polonius' body: "I'll lug the guts into the neighbour room." Again he bids Gertrude goodnight.

Commentary

It is upon this scene in particular that the neo-Freudians depend for support of their explanation of Hamlet's conduct, since here the tragic hero does reveal an overwhelming concern about Gertrude's sexual life. They find in this scene a Hamlet moved not by idealism and family honor, but by consuming jealousy due to his unconscious, incestuous love for his mother. For them, Hamlet's hatred of Claudius results from the fact that Claudius—rather than Hamlet himself—killed the king. In contrast to the neo-Freudians, the orthodox Shakespeareans, who never forget that Shakespeare was a man of the Renaissance, find in this scene a Hamlet who is a moral idealist and who neither exaggerates Gertrude's guilt nor indulges in self-righteousness.

Up to this scene, the extent of Gertrude's guilt has not been made clear. Now it may be concluded that she knew nothing about the murder of King Hamlet. She is shocked when Hamlet draws his sword and drives the blade through the arras, killing Polonius. But her horror and surprise are just as great when Hamlet picks up her words and goes on to condemn her.

To paraphrase the ghost's words when it first spoke to Hamlet, Gertrude is the "weak vessel," deficient in moral insight and therefore susceptible to the persuasion of Claudius. This estimate of her character finds support when her son, directing her to look upon the portraits of King Hamlet and Claudius, asks: "Ha! have you eyes?". Only with reluctance can she move just a step toward moral awareness and self-criticism:

> O, speak to me no more.
> These words like daggers enter in mine ears.
> No more, sweet Hamlet.
>
> (Act III, Sc. 4, 96-98)

Although she assures the prince that she will not breathe a word of what has been said, she does not promise to avoid further intimacy with Claudius. When the ghost appears to Hamlet, Gertrude exclaims: "Alas, he's mad!". Under the circumstances, her reaction is a natural one; but this may serve to relieve her of the tormenting belief that Hamlet spoke truly to her, however cruelly. Her conduct in subsequent scenes tends to support such a conclusion.

The range of emotions which Hamlet exhibits in this scene is great. After concluding the "shenting" of Gertrude with a cutting condemnation of "the bloat king," he practically gloats over the prospect of out-smarting Rosencrantz and Guildenstern, the willing servants of Claudius.

The Hamlet we see in this scene is far from being "A man that fortune's buffets and rewards" takes "with equal thanks," but rather one who is prepared to "drink hot blood." However aware one is that Hamlet has "great cause," one should not ignore the fact that he is far from the ideal he declared Horatio to be earlier.

Many of the prince's lines seem to be as cruel as those he addressed to Ophelia in the nunnery scene, although the motivation is sounder since he has sprung the Mouse-trap and is addressing a mother whose conduct is immoral. From the start, his tone is harsh enough to make Gertrude fear for her life. (There is no textual evidence that he threatens her with physical violence; the traditional stage directions indicate that he draws his sword only when he hears Polonius cry out from behind the arras.) "How now! A rat?" he asks—and one is reminded of the Mouse-trap set for Claudius. After discovering that he has killed the elderly lord chamberlain, his remarks are unfeeling:

> Thou wretched, rash, intruding fool, farewell!
> I took thee for thy better. Take thy fortune.
> Thou find'st to be too busy is some danger.
>
> (Act III, Sc. 4, 31-33)

Turning to Gertrude, Hamlet says coldly: "Leave wringing of your hands."

In the preceding scene, Hamlet had been restrained from killing his uncle-king only by a determination not only to take the life of his adversary but also to insure Claudius' damnation. Now, acting impulsively, he strikes with his sword, convinced that its blade will reach the king. Would a subdued, rational Hamlet be satisfied that his motive for revenge was not colored by a personal hatred outweighing public duty? This is a question which should not be ignored. So intense is Hamlet's detestation of Claudius that, in this scene, his bitter words match those he used in the first and second soliloquies; but here they are intensified. Claudius is not only "A king of shreds and patches;" he is the "bloat king," a "paddock [toad] ," a "bat," and a "gib [tomcat]." The bestial images are used to represent extreme, disgusting sensuality.

All this is developed most effectively when Hamlet calls upon Gertrude to look at the pictures, the "counterfeit presentment of two brothers." His words relate back to two important, earlier passages in the play: his first soliloquy and his advice to the players. In the soliloquy, the prince provided the initial contrast between his father and Claudius. (See Act I, Sc. 2, 139-40, 152-53.) In his advice to the players, Hamlet urged them not to overstep "the modesty of nature" but rather to hold "the mirror up to nature," showing "virtue her own feature, scorn her own image." To Hamlet, Claudius, whose portrait contrasts so unfavorably with that of the dead ruler, imitates humanity monstrously. "This was your husband," he tells his mother, comparing the dead King to the four gods of the classical Pantheon; and then he directs her attention to the picture of Claudius: "Here is your husband, like a mildew'd ear,/Blasting his wholesome brother." When the prince goes on to compare Claudius to a "moor" upon which Gertrude now "battens" (gorges herself), he is strongly emphasizing appetite as opposed to reason.

Hamlet had ended his first soliloquy with a lament: "But break my heart, for I must hold my tongue." The antic disposition did give him opportunities to express his heartfelt thoughts, but never directly to his mother and only rarely to his uncle-king. Having sprung the Mouse-trap and proved to his own satisfaction that Claudius, once an object of scorn but now the powerful ruler of Denmark, is guilty of regicide, he need not suffer in silence. Claudius now is fully aware that Hamlet has discovered his secret; in the dramatization of *The Murder of Gonzago* he saw a portrait of himself. It is now Gertrude's turn to see her true image.

In the mature works of Shakespeare (as elsewhere in much of the serious literature of the period), illicit sex was a symbol of pervading evil. Hamlet's apparent obsession with the sensual, amounts to what has been called sexual nausea. Consider the prince's reply to Gertrude when she asks why he belittles her:

                              Such an act
That blurs the grace and blush of modesty,
Calls virtue hypocrite, takes off the rose
From the fair forehead of an innocent love
And sets a blister there, makes marriage vows
As false as dicers' oaths.

                              (Act III, Sc. IV, 41-46)

"Sets a blister," as here used, means "brands as a harlot." One immediately recalls the nunnery scene. The lord chamberlain's daughter had been "loosed" upon Hamlet, and to him she was not "honest"; in a sense, she was being prostituted by an unprincipled father in the service of Claudius. Yet he surely knew that Ophelia was a helpless victim. The source of the corruption was the king, who had won over Gertrude as a partner in an unholy union. This was an act which the idealistic Christian prince finds to be so monstrous that it reflects on mankind, and especially man's brave claim to being the paragon of animals.

Hamlet indeed has spoken "daggers" to Gertrude. But when the ghost appears and not only rebukes him for procrastination but also urges him to "step between [Gertrude] and her fighting soul." Hamlet seems to be aware that he has violated the ghost's earlier warning by striving against his mother, instead of leaving her to heaven. Not without compassion, he now begs her not to interpret his words as evidence of madness and thus an excuse for her to ignore her guilt. Rather, let her confess herself to heaven, or at the very least avoid compounding her sin by going to Claudius' bed.

In this calmer mood, the prince now can express repentance for the killing of Polonius and declare that he will report the deed honestly. Yet his words are of special interest:

                    . . . but heaven hath pleased it so,
To punish me with this, and this with me,
That I must be their scourge and minister.
                              (Act III, Sc. 4, 173-76)

A scourge is a wicked person who adds to his evil deeds even while functioning as the instrument of God's vengeance; ultimately he will fall and will endure eternal damnation. A minister is the virtuous instrument of God's justice. Is it possible for anyone to be both scourge and minister? Among many theories advanced by Shakespearean critics, this question is as important as any other one. It is quite possible that Shakespeare intends to show that the tragic hero himself is still in doubt regarding the morality of the task which remains to be performed. Hamlet's words in the present scene illuminate the dilemma he has faced practically from the start: is it possible to accept as a moral duty the execution of revenge upon Claudius without tainting his own mind? Should he be the Pyrrhus-type revenger, the man of blood and passion, prompt in action, unrestrained by the processes of thought?

Finally, the ghost in this scene demands attention, especially because this time only Hamlet sees it. First, why does it make its last appearance at this particular place and only to one of the two persons present? A widely accepted theory is that it does so because Hamlet is doing something that he should not do—speaking daggers to the woman who should be left to heaven. Such an action, so the argument goes, would be proper for the spirit of the Hyperion-like King Hamlet; moreover, it would be the action of a benevolent spirit, an "honest" ghost. But it also has been argued that, since Gertrude does not see or hear the ghost and therefore believes her son to be mad, the ghost's appearance only to Hamlet defeats her intention to repent. If this reading is valid, then the ghost may be evil. When the prince first sees it, he exclaims: "Save me, and hover o'er me with your wings,/You heavenly guards!" This is a variation of the orthodox Christian formula to be used when one sees a ghost. One may reasonably ask why he should use this formula if he really is convinced that this is "a spirit of health," not a "goblin damn'd." Still another theory is that Gertrude cannot see the ghost because she is a sinner.

An indisputable reason for the ghost's appearance, acknowledged by Hamlet and confirmed by the ghost itself, is to reprove the prince for delaying the revenge. Just possibly its appearance may be due to Hamlet's failure to take advantage of the opportunity when Claudius knelt in an attempt to pray. However, one may well ask: would a good spirit have approved of action under such circumstances? Other commentators point out another disturbing possibility. Perhaps Hamlet, in a state of great passion, is actually experiencing a hallucination, the reflection of his own state of mind. Although this theory is not generally accepted, it cannot be dismissed. The startled prince addresses the ghost in these words:

> Do you not come your tardy son to chide,
> That, laps'd in time and passion, lets go by
> Th' important acting of your dread command?
> (Act III, Sc. 4, 107-109)

These words of self-accusation, it has been argued, are motivated by Hamlet's failure to kill Claudius when he had his chance shortly after springing the Mouse-trap. Further, Hamlet repeats in essence just what he said about himself earlier, when he denounced himself as being "A dull and muddy-mettled rascal . . . unpregnant of [his] cause" and referred to his "weakness" and his "melancholy," and also in his third soliloquy when he spoke of the "native hue of resolution" being "sicklied o'er with the pale cast of thought." Consistent with this argument is the ghost's reply: "Do not forget! This visitation/Is but to whet thy almost blunted purpose."

ACT IV • SCENE 1

Summary

Claudius expresses concern for the emotionally disturbed Gertrude and asks where her son is. First dismissing Rosencrantz and Guildenstern, the queen replies that Hamlet, "Mad as the sea and wind, when both contend/Which is the mightier," has killed Polonius, the "unseen good old man." The king laments the violent deed, aware that he would have been the victim had he been behind the arras. Accusing himself of negligence for not restraining Hamlet earlier, he wonders how he will be able to explain Polonius' death to his subjects. Gertrude informs him that the prince, regretting his action, is removing the body of the lord chamberlain.

The king states that Hamlet must be sent away at once, and he calls for Guildenstern. When the latter enters with Rosencrantz, the two are told what has happened and instructed to seek out Hamlet, talk with him as if nothing had occurred, and bring Polonius' body to the chapel. They depart. Claudius then informs Gertrude that they must turn to their wisest friends and tell them what they "mean to do/And what's untimely done." Perhaps then they will not be held accountable for the death of Polonius.

Commentary

Gertrude's explanation of what happened has been subject to contrasting interpretations. To most readers, it seems evident that she honestly believes her son to be mad because she speaks of his grief as evidence of his basic purity, and because Claudius' lines point to his awareness of her genuine love and concern for her son. Others see Gertrude as making good her promise not to reveal Hamlet's secret, but as having accepted eagerly the belief that he is mentally unbalanced as a "flattering unction to [her] soul," to use the prince's own words.

Claudius' words and actions in this scene pose no such problem of interpretation. In the course of the action so far in this play, his concern for his own security has been linked to Hamlet. The behavior of Hamlet now has become an obsession with him. "Ah, my good lord, what I have seen tonight!" exclaims Gertrude, and Claudius promptly asks, "How does Hamlet?" And, at the end of the scene, he says, "My soul is full of discord and dismay." But, with Machiavellian skill, he expresses his conviction that Hamlet is now a threat not only to the crown, but also to all subjects; and he blames himself for permitting his "love" for the prince to interfere with duty. The intensity of the conflict is perhaps best indicated by the king's use of a military figure of speech when he tells Gertrude how they must report the death of Polonius.

Finally, it now seems possible that Hamlet's killing of Polonius has worked to the advantage of Claudius. Only select members of the court witnessed Hamlet's antic behavior and heard his deranged speech. The prince, who, as Ophelia earlier made clear, was the "expectancy and rose of the fair state," can now be removed from Denmark without causing subjects to ask troublesome questions.

ACT IV • SCENE 2

Summary

Hamlet, adopting the same ironic and riddling style of conversation which he used earlier, refuses to tell Rosencrantz and Guildenstern where he placed the body of Polonius, but he agrees to go with them to see the king.

Commentary

Why Hamlet chooses to irritate the king and his spies by hiding Polonius' body is a bit of a puzzle. Many find here a perverseness unworthy of a tragic hero; others find further evidence of the prince's preoccupation with death, first revealed in his soliloquy at the end of Act I, Scene 2, and developed in the "To be, or not to be" soliloquy in Act III, Scene 1.

The prince's contempt for Rosencrantz and Guildenstern finds expression once more. Speaking to the former, he explains Rosencrantz' motive for serving Claudius: this former schoolfellow is a sponge that "soaks up the king's countenance [reference to the coin of the realm], his rewards, his authorities;" like other servile individuals, the king keeps him "as an ape doth nuts, in the corner of his jaw; first mouth'd, to be last swallowed." Having listened to Rosencrantz and Guildenstern speak about the sanctity of kingship, one is hardly surprised that Guildenstern should express shock when he hears Hamlet refer to the king as a "thing."

ACT IV • SCENE 3

Summary

Addressing a small group of courtiers, Claudius states that he has sent for Hamlet, who must not be confined, despite his dangerous lunacy, because the "distracted multitude," lacking true judgment, love him. The decision to exile Hamlet must be represented as the verdict of the wisest counselors. Rosencrantz enters and reports that Hamlet will not reveal what he has done with Polonius' body. In response to the king's command, he calls to Guildenstern to bring in the prince.

Questioned by the king, Hamlet replies with witty, cynical remarks but tells him nothing. Finally, he states that Polonius' body may be found if one goes "up the stairs into the lobby." When told that he must be sent to England, Hamlet continues to bait the king, bidding him "Farewell, dear mother."

After Hamlet has left, Claudius orders Rosencrantz and Guildenstern to see to it that the prince is aboard ship by nightfall. Left to himself, Claudius then voices his thoughts: Hamlet is to be put to death as soon as he arrives in England; only then can Claudius find repose.

Commentary

Hamlet seems to take great satisfaction in his pretended madness; but, if anything, his wit is grimmer than ever. Again he seems to be completely morbid in his preoccupation with death. Questioned about Polonius' body, he develops the "worm's meat" theme, inherited by the Renaissance from the Middle Ages. However high-spirited Hamlet may seem, however unfeeling in his attitude toward the dead Polonius, this is the same Hamlet who, after his moving tribute to mankind as "the beauty of the world," asked, "And yet, to me, what is this quintessence of dust?"—and then went on to declare that man did not please him. It is the same Hamlet who was at least half in love with death when he voiced his thoughts in the "To be, or not to be" soliloquy. It is Hamlet the disillusioned idealist who has discovered how low man may sink. So now he gets a perverse pleasure out of telling Claudius that

> A certain convocation of politic [politically-minded] worms are e'en at him [Polonius]. Your worm is your only emperor for diet. We fat all creatures else to fat us, and we fat ourselves for maggots. Your fat king and your learn beggar is but variable service—two dishes, but to one table. That's the end.
> (Act IV, Sc. 3, 19-25)

In the development of the "worm's meat" theme during the Middle Ages, the aim was to teach the religious lesson that heaven should be recognized as man's destination and ultimate home, and that he should not be misled by whatever life on earth has to offer. But there is no consolation of religion in Hamlet's grim remarks; the whole emphasis is upon man's insignificance. It would be advisable to keep this episode in mind when one comes to the graveyard scene in the last act.

Finally, Hamlet bids farewell to the king, calling him his mother and going on to explain, "Father and mother is man and wife, man and wife is one flesh [as they are called in Scripture], and so, my mother." One is reminded that the cause of Hamlet's tragedy is twofold. Never does he forget his father's death; but the incestuous marriage continues to torment him.

ACT IV • SCENE 4

Summary

Fortinbras leads his army across a plain in Denmark. He leaves a captain to greet Claudius and get his approval for the march through Danish territory. Hamlet, escorted by Rosencrantz and Guildenstern, appears and questions the captain. He learns that the Norwegian soldiers are about to fight with the Poles over "a little patch of ground" which is practically worthless. Requesting his escort to move ahead, the prince pauses to reflect upon what he has just learned. He sees in Fortinbras' determined move against the Poles another lesson to himself. True greatness, he concludes, means to act decisively when honor is the issue. Yet he, whose father has been murdered and whose mother has been morally corrupted, has let time lapse without taking revenge upon Claudius. From now on, his "thoughts [will] be bloody, or be nothing worth!"

Commentary

In this scene Hamlet soliloquizes at length for the last time. Some critics have described this soliloquy as Hamlet's most decisive one in that it puts an end to doubt and hesitation. Hamlet's comparison of himself to Fortinbras has been widely recognized as thematic, and there are some commentators who insist that the young Norwegian prince is the most important foil to Hamlet in this play. Like the prince of Denmark, he has lost a royal father and is intent on seeking prompt revenge, for which purpose he has raised his army of "landless resolutes." He had planned to invade Denmark, but, thanks to Claudius' diplomatic efforts, the ruler of Norway was persuaded to attack Poland instead. It has been argued that Fortinbras, unlike Hamlet, has mastered passion, adopted the principles of reason, yet does not lapse into inactivity. From this point of view, he does provide a contrast to Hamlet. The difficulty, however, lies in the immediate reason given for Fortinbras' decision to fight the Polish forces. Does Hamlet mean that it is "divine ambition" which makes the Norwegian prince dare "fortune, death, and danger," knowing that some twenty thousand men probably will be slaughtered for all what he deems to be an honorable cause? Surely this cannot be the case, as Hamlet's next lines, properly understood, indicate:

> Rightly to be great
> Is not to stir without great argument,
> But greatly to find quarrel in a straw
> When honor's at the stake.
>
> (Act IV, Sc. 4, 53-56)

The only example which Fortinbras provides Hamlet relates to his prompt action, without thoughts of consequences. Hamlet's own reason for acting—his "quarrel" (argument)—is not in "a straw," nor is the act of upholding family honor and punishing the crimes of Claudius an "egg-shell."

But what of the most impressively philosophical lines in this soliloquy?

> What is a man,
> If his chief good and market of his time
> Be but to sleep and feed? A beast, no more.
> Sure He that made us with such large discourse,
> Looking before and after, gave us not
> That capability and godlike reason
> To fust in us unus'd.
>
> (Act IV, Sc. 4, 33-39)

These lines relate to Hamlet's "What a piece of work is a man" speech and enlarge upon what he said then: man is endowed with reason and must put this divine gift to use through positive action. Hamlet goes on to accuse himself of either "Bestial oblivion" or "Of thinking too precisely on th' event," arguing that "thought which, quarter'd, hath but one part wisdom/And ever three parts coward." This is the passage upon which the Romantics, including Goethe and Coleridge especially, depend to justify their concept of Hamlet as the inactive dreamer. It may be argued that "thinking too precisely on th' event" would mean to reject effective reason, and that it is better to have only one-fourth wisdom than to try to solve momentous questions with none at all. If all this be true, then one may conclude that Shakespeare is particularly interested in working toward a precise definition of the moral issue which his tragic hero faces.

And what is to be made of the following lines spoken by Hamlet after he has accused himself of cowardice?

> . . . I do not know
> Why yet I live to say, 'This thing's to do,'
> Sith I have cause and will and strength and means
> To do't.
>
> (Act IV, Sc. 4, 43-46)

This is exactly the temper of the Hamlet who soliloquized "O, what a rogue and peasant slave am I!" and of the Hamlet of the "To be, or not to be" soliloquy. In the brief time that has elapsed since he sprang the Mouse-trap, Hamlet has had one real opportunity to kill Claudius, but he does know *why* he failed to do so. Understandably, some commentators suggest that this soliloquy has been misplaced; but it is more logical to conclude that the prince has been emotionally aroused by just what he says—one more "occasion" reminding him that after many months the King survives and rules Denmark with Gertrude as his "imperial jointress."

"O, from this time forth,/My thoughts be bloody, or be nothing worth!" the prince concludes. His thoughts were sufficiently bloody when he spoke the lines of his second soliloquy, and certainly when he came upon the kneeling Claudius shortly after he had sprung the Mouse-trap. Perhaps Fortinbras' single-minded pursuit of his goal has provided Hamlet with an example, which will make it possible for him to act positively and promptly if an opportunity presents itself. So full of self-reproach is he now that apparently the end will justify whatever means he can find. In part, such a conclusion is supported by the fact that this scene leads to the final, larger movement in the play, one in which the tragic hero no longer will have the need to express his doubts and perplexities.

ACT IV • SCENE 5

Summary

A court gentleman informs Gertrude that Ophelia seems to be out of her mind and in her pitiable state has become troublesome. Gertrude flatly states that she will not see her. When the gentleman tells how Ophelia speaks constantly of her father and behaves in a most unusual manner, Horatio points out that her wild talk may arouse suspicion. Gertrude then agrees to see her.

Ophelia enters, asks for "the beauteous majesty of Denmark," talks incoherently, and sings verses of ballads, one obviously relating thematically to the death of her elderly father, the other two relating to the seduction of an innocent maiden. Claudius, who has joined the group, addresses her graciously but receives no rational reply. He is convinced that her father's death has driven her mad. When she leaves, he orders that she be closely watched. He then turns to Gertrude and summarizes the troubles in Elsinore: Polonius is dead; Hamlet is no longer in the kingdom; the body of the lord chamberlain has been hastily and secretly buried; the king's subjects are suspicious and increasingly restless; Laertes, returned in secret from France, has been upset by unwholesome rumors. Claudius is in a state of torment.

Loud noises are heard, and the king calls for his soldiers to guard the door, just as a messenger enters to report that Laertes and a mob who hail him as Claudius' successor have overcome officers of the guard and are about to break in. That is exactly what happens. But Laertes orders his followers to take up a position outside the room and then addresses the king and queen, demanding that they "give" him his father. Gertrude urges him to calm down, but it is the diplomatic Claudius who succeeds in reasoning with Laertes.

Ophelia returns, again singing snatches of a ballad, the words of which relate to the sad death of a man with "beard as white as snow," and again talking incoherently. In fantasy, she distributes various flowers to those who watch and listen to her. Laertes is beside himself with grief for his "kind sister, sweet Ophelia." When Ophelia leaves, Claudius succeeds in getting Laertes' attention. He promises to join Laertes in punishing the guilty in the matter of Polonius' death.

Commentary

The irony in this scene is quite striking. Ophelia has spoken of Hamlet's mind as being "o'erthrown," but it is she who is now genuinely mad. Some have raised the question of whether her madness, so distressing since she has been no more than the dutiful daughter of a vain and foolish father, is necessary to the plot. One critic, for example, argues that Laertes has motive enough to act as he does without his sister's madness, which he calls a "dramatic luxury" (L. L. Schücking, *Character Problems in Shakespeare's Plays*). Further, if one is convinced that Hamlet should have left Claudius, as well as Gertrude, to heaven (in which case the ghost is an evil spirit intent on leading Hamlet to his destruction), Ophelia's madness and subsequent death result from "the frightening process of a course that never should have been initiated" (E. Prosser, *Hamlet and Revenge*). The consensus is that Ophelia's madness and death have a logical place in the entire action because they coincide with, and illustrate, one result of disorder in the state—the rottenness which has been spreading through the ruling body.

The second tragic love song sung by Ophelia, beginning with "To-morrow is Saint Valentine's day" and concluding with "And thou hadst not come to my bed," has intrigued many commentators. Those who read the play primarily as a romantic love tragedy involving Hamlet and Ophelia recall that Ophelia has already spoken of having "suck'd the honey of his music vows" and are convinced that Hamlet has had his way with Ophelia and then rejected her. For some of these romantics, this is the primary cause of her mental collapse, the death of her father being the secondary cause.

What is the justification for having Ophelia sing a song, the theme of which is the seduction and abandonment of an innocent maiden? It will be recalled that the suspicious Polonius had instructed his daughter not to be so naïve as to think that the prince would marry her—not to be misled by Hamlet's courting her in what she reported as honorable fashion. It has also been pointed out that illicit sex in Shakespeare's later dramas is repeatedly used as a symbol of pervading evil. All this adds up to one conclusion: Ophelia's song is intended to underscore the destructive force of evil in the kingdom. And the source of the infection is Claudius. Ophelia is the latest victim; little wonder, then, that she should sing of "despised love." Nor is this conclusion inconsistent with the claim that Hamlet's harsh words to her in the nunnery scene planted the image of illicit sex in her mind.

Ophelia's distribution of the flowers (perhaps imaginary, although her first words in the First Quarto after her return are "Wel God a mercy, I a bin gathering of floures.") is of some interest in terms of symbolism. To her brother she gives rosemary, which was used at both weddings and funerals as a symbol of remembrance. It may be her impending death, not just that of Polonius, that is symbolized here; if so, her words are indeed "A document in madness," as Laertes says. Pansies, which she also gives to Laertes, symbolize thoughts, and therefore are no less appropriate. Apparently the fennel, representing flattery, is given to the king, and the columbines, symbolizing thanklessness, to the queen. To Gertrude also are given the rue and daisy, the first ("herb of grace") symbolizes sorrow, and the second may represent a warning to women who are too easily persuaded to love. Neither Gertrude nor Claudius is given violets, which stand for faithfulness.

In this scene, it is Laertes who emerges as a foil to Hamlet. He has been stirred by "great argument," to use the phrase from the prince's last soliloquy. Like Hamlet, he has lost a beloved father, one who was murdered. When the ghost concluded its account of King Hamlet's murder, it called upon Hamlet to prove that he had "nature" (natural feelings) in him by avenging his father's death. There is no question regarding such nature in Laertes, who is not to be restrained in his determination to prove that he is his father's son. Laertes is "stirred" to uphold the honor of his family. After the news of his father's death reached him in Paris, he left for Elsinore; now he has burst into the room and threatens the king. Laertes, it would seem, is the model avenger for a tragedy of blood. He will act first and act promptly, undisturbed by questions of public duty, morality, or consequences:

> I dare damnation. To this point I stand,
> That both the worlds I give to negligence,
> Let come what comes, only I'll be revenged
> Most throughly for my father.
>
> (Act IV, Sc. 5, 133-36)

There is little danger of conscience making a coward of Laertes or of his thinking too precisely on the event. In his own way, he is as single-minded as Fortinbras, who is determined to fight over "a little patch of ground," whatever the cost in human lives may be.

When Laertes first sees Ophelia, now deranged, the tenderness of the meeting is not to be denied. Yet his speech beginning "O heat, dry up my brains!" is sufficiently artificial in style to suggest that the player describing the grief of Hecuba might well have recited it. Perhaps all this may seem to be too harsh a criticism of a youth who loved and was loyal to the members of his family, one who was especially concerned that his father had been denied proper burial and honors appropriate for a lord chamberlain. But the point is that, although he too may serve as a foil to Hamlet, he is anything but a norm character.

Before leaving the discussion of Laertes in this scene, one should call attention to the fact that he was able to raise a rebellion of sorts. It is reasonable to ask why Hamlet, whose popularity was established by the testimony of Ophelia and that of Claudius, did not secure public support in a revolt against the king. Some have believed that he could have succeeded in deposing Claudius, and even had the King brought to trial for regicide. All this, of course, would have entailed a drastic revision of the original story elements. Moreover, in Shakespeare's play, evidence of political discontent and disorder has been presented only after the death of Polonius.

Close attention to the lines spoken by Claudius makes clear how intense the conflict in this play has become. "O Gertrude, Gertrude," says the guilt-ridden King. "When sorrows come, they come not single spies,/But in battalions." Of course he is striving to sustain the public image of a virtuous ruler and concerned kinsman of a prince who, in his madness, has disrupted an orderly realm. Actually Claudius is an increasingly fearful individual. But he remains a strong opponent; there is no danger that he will collapse or suddenly abandon the conflict. He is still the capable Machiavellian, gifted in pretense and prompt in action. In this role, Claudius achieves supreme irony when he speaks of "poor Ophelia" and when he urges Gertrude not to restrain the enraged Laertes:

> Let him go, Gertrude. Do not fear our person.
> There's such divinity doth hedge a king
> That treason can but peep to what it would, . . .
> (Act IV, Sc. 5, 122-24)

This is the public image of a ruler which the competent Claudius has presented, although one may agree with Hamlet that he is actually "a king of shreds and patches." No one is likely to underestimate his skill when he succeeds in calming Laertes' anger, assuring the lord chamberlain's son that, if he (Claudius) is found to be to blame in any degree, he will give up both his kingdom and life, and promising that Laertes will be given complete satisfaction: "And where th' offense is, let the great axe fall." When one comes to the final scene, the resolution of this tragedy, these words will be recognized as ironic; but immediately they reveal the king not only saving himself from the immediate threat posed by Laertes' revolt, but also capitalizing upon that very turn of events. If Hamlet is put to death in accordance with Claudius' instructions, the members of the court and, one may assume, the public at large, convinced by Claudius that he has become a homicidal maniac, will not be "Thick and unwholesome in their thoughts and whispers," to use the king's own words.

ACT IV • SCENE 6

Summary
Horatio is told by his attendant that some sailors wish to give him certain letters. Aware that he knows of no one except Hamlet who might have written to him, he immediately instructs the attendant to let the sailors enter. From the letter, Horatio learns that the ship bearing Hamlet to England was attacked by pirates. During the fight, Hamlet boarded the pirate ship and was made captive. He was well-treated and brought back to Denmark in return for his promise to do them a good turn. Horatio is to deliver the other letters to the king and then come to Hamlet without delay, for he has much to tell his friend. Horatio promises to reward the sailors when they have guided him to the prince.

Commentary
This scene pictures Hamlet as alert, determined and active in escaping, and in dealing with the pirates. It also arouses curiosity as to what has become of Rosencrantz and Guildenstern.

The sailors, it is sufficiently clear, are some of the pirates who detained Hamlet and then returned him to Denmark. The return of Hamlet is a plain indication that the resolution of the entire action is not far off.

ACT IV • SCENE 7

Summary
The king has told Laertes that Hamlet killed Polonius and sought to kill him, Claudius. When Laertes asks why the king did not have the prince punished for such capital offences, Claudius explains that he did not do so for two reasons: first, the queen dotes upon her son and, devoted as he is to her, he restrained himself; second, he could not expect support from the public, who reveres Hamlet. He assures Laertes that he never considered letting the prince escape punishment.

At this point a messenger enters with letters from Hamlet, one for the king and one for the queen. From his letter, Claudius learns that the prince has returned to Denmark. Immediately the king proceeds to involve Laertes in a plot to kill Hamlet. The king tells him how Hamlet's sense of rivalry was aroused by the report of Laertes' skill in fencing. Laertes, he says, can prove that he loved his father by taking advantage of this situation as a means of avenging Polonius' death without risking injury to himself. When Laertes declares that nothing could restrain him from acting against Hamlet, Claudius tells him that he will arrange a fencing match between the two and that Laertes will use a foil with an unblunted point. Laertes then can kill Hamlet before the eyes of the spectators without appearing to intend any harm. Laertes not only agrees but plans to go beyond this: he will dip the point of his sword in deadly poison. Claudius adds a second means of insuring Hamlet's death. He will have available a cup of poisoned wine for Hamlet to drink if Laertes somehow fails to draw blood in the duel.

Gertrude enters, lamenting. She informs Laertes that his sister is drowned. Both he and Claudius learn that, while Ophelia was weaving fantastic garlands and hanging them on the limbs of a willow tree, a limb broke and she fell into the stream. For a brief time she floated, then she sank to her death. Laertes strives to control his grief but cannot do so. When he leaves, Claudius tells Gertrude that now he must begin once more the task of calming Laertes' rage.

Commentary

Repeatedly, Claudius has been described as Machiavellian in his villainy. But it also has been pointed out that, unlike the usual Machiavellian villain of the Elizabethan stage, he suffers the pangs of conscience and is not the heartless schemer who scoffs at religion and gloats over his own wickedness. As one definitely learns in this scene, he is genuinely fond of Gertrude, and this capacity for love is another characteristic which differentiates him from the completely dedicated Machiavellian. In other respects—cunning, capacity for cruelty, wisdom however misdirected—Claudius, especially in this scene, can take his place at the side of Richard III, Iago, Edmund, and other stage villains who in many ways, if not all, are Machiavellian types.

In winning over Laertes, the last and most formidable agent he uses against Hamlet, Claudius succeeds in presenting himself as a ruler who has failed to act for a reason which reflects favorably upon his character. Although he acknowledges the fact that his nephew is popular, he is astute enough not to mention that, as he had said in an earlier scene, the prince is "lov'd by the distracted multitude." It is also characteristic of him that he should formulate a plan which, if executed properly, will not involve much risk:

> And for his death no wind of blame shall breathe,
> But even his mother shall uncharge the practice
> And call it accident.

(Act IV, Sc. 7, 65-67)

This, of course, is the practical, clever way in which "Diseases desperate grown" are relieved in a world where "seeming" and "acting" are a way of life. There is, then, a certain logic, even inevitability, in the choice of poison for the purpose of killing Hamlet: it was poison which

Claudius used to gain his crown and wife; poison began the whole process of this villainy.

Claudius' Machiavellianism is evident not only in his prompt approval of Laertes' plan to use a foil tipped with poison, but also in planning to have the poisoned drink ready, should Laertes fail. To some extent, it is also evident in his report that the Norman horseman had the highest praise for Laertes' skill in swordsmanship and that Hamlet became envious when he heard Laertes praised. And so, when, having learned that Hamlet has_ returned to Denmark alone and "naked" (unarmed), Claudius asks Laertes: "Can you advise me?" Perhaps Claudius knows very well that modesty is not a notable trait in Polonius' son and certainly he knows that flattery can be an effective device.

Laertes remains the "perfect" avenger, one not to be stopped by anything. But now there is a great falling off in his character. Whatever his limitations may have been before, he invited great sympathy. His cause was great: a father killed and denied a decent funeral, his sister driven mad. It is not just that he is easily won over by Claudius. Rather, it is that he is the one who, even prior to listening to Claudius' plan, intended to use a sword with a poisoned tip. One can only conclude that he is his father's son and cannot be wholly above-board. But the issue now is one of life and death. Admittedly, Laertes recovers one's sympathy after he learns of Ophelia's death, especially because, in contrast to the ranting style he used when he saw and heard his demented sister in Act IV, Scene 5, he now speaks moving words and is impressively restrained. Nevertheless, it is this report of Ophelia's death that seals the pact between Laertes and Claudius.

When Claudius asks Laertes if his father was dear to him, one recalls the ghost's words to Hamlet: "If thou didst ever thy dear father love—" and its command that Hamlet prove his love: "Revenge his foul and most unnatural murder." Audience and reader alike are reminded that the prince has delayed; months have elapsed, yet Claudius survives as king of Denmark. Among those who accept Hamlet's self-indictment for not sweeping to his revenge, this entire episode is called upon to support their interpretation. It would seem more reasonable to conclude that throughout this scene, in which he does not appear, Hamlet emerges as the admirable tragic hero, despite delays and rationalizations for them. Claudius acknowledges him to be "Most generous and free from all contriving." It follows that, although procrastination made possible what has been called the "increase in the area of destruction," the prince himself is the victim of his superior morality: his very virtues work to his disadvantage in the corrupt world in which he finds himself. Laertes surely could use considerable "thinking . . . precisely on th' event," the tendency which Hamlet felt might be the cause of his failure to carry out the ghost's command. And when Laertes declares his willingness to cut Hamlet's throat in the church, he obviously could use some of Hamlet's moral scruples. But even here, it may be pointed out that when Laertes makes his wild statement, one is reminded of Hamlet's refusal to kill Claudius as the latter knelt for prayer. One also recalls that the prince was motivated not by religious duty but by a determination to obtain "perfect" revenge. Yet, in the balance, the prince of Denmark emerges as admirable. He could no more seek to avenge his father's death in the way adopted by Laertes than he could imitate Fortinbras in leading troops to slaughter for the sake of a worthless patch of ground.

"One woe doth tread upon another's heel,/ So fast they follow," says Gertrude as Ophelia's sad death by drowning is revealed. The rottenness in the state of Denmark, present from the beginning of this play, has spread. The tragic course of events has been gaining increasing momentum and has reached this crucial point at the end of Act IV. Gertrude's touching description of Ophelia's death is a setpiece. That it is appropriate to the queen has been questioned; but the Gertrude who has emerged as genuinely devoted to her son surely is capable of sincere grief for the death of Ophelia. More relevant is the fact that, from Gertrude's report, Ophelia's death was accidental, not suicide, a fact that poses a minor problem in view of the dispute in the next scene regarding her burial.

ACT V • SCENE 1

Summary
Two gravediggers discuss the recent inquest of the death of Ophelia, held to determine whether or not she was a suicide and whether or not she merits a Christian burial. The first gravedigger is convinced that she will be accorded that privilege only because she is a gentlewoman.

While the second gravedigger goes to fetch a pot of liquor, Hamlet and Horatio enter, pausing to listen to the first gravedigger as he sings snatches of a ballad and digs in the earth. When he tosses up a skull and dashes it to the ground, the prince begins to reflect upon death as the great leveler of all people. He then questions the first gravedigger, who answers him in chop-logic, a particular kind of speech in which the speaker insists upon confining himself to a special meaning of a given word or phrase. In reply to a question, the gravedigger states that he has followed his calling since the day when King Hamlet defeated old King Fortinbras of Norway, on which day young Hamlet ("he that was mad, and sent into England") was born—thirty years ago, so he says.

Hamlet questions him further. The gravedigger identifies the skull as that of Yorick, the king's jester, who died twenty-three years ago. Hamlet picks it up and tells Horatio that Yorick was his childhood favorite. Now once more he dwells upon death, which brings not only a court jester to this state but also the vain court lady and even great conquerors like Alexander the Great and Caesar, whose dust may now fill a crack in a wall.

As the funeral procession enters, the members of which include the king, the queen, and Laertes, Hamlet and Horatio step back, unobserved. Laertes complains to the priest about the limited rites accorded his dead sister. The priest insists that Ophelia is being accorded rites which she really does not deserve in view of the doubtful circumstances of her death.

When Ophelia's body is lowered into the grave, the queen strews the coffin with flowers and speaks touchingly of her defeated hope that Ophelia would have become Hamlet's wife. Laertes, no longer able to restrain himself, cries out in grief and then leaps into the grave, asking that he be buried with his sister. At this point in the action, Hamlet steps forth and demands to know why Laertes should so emphasize his sorrow. Announcing himself as "Hamlet, the Dane," he too leaps into the grave. Laertes seizes him by the throat, and the two grapple until they are separated by attendants and then climb out of the grave.

Horatio attempts to calm the prince, but the latter is not to be silenced. He declares that he loved Ophelia far more than Laertes could have loved her, bitterly criticizes Laertes for indulging in pompous speech-making, and then insists that he has always held him in high esteem. Gertrude again expresses her belief that her son is mad. After Hamlet leaves, Claudius speaks to Laertes, reminding him that he has not long to wait for vengeance.

Commentary

In the first act, Claudius, addressing the assembled court, had spoken of "mirth in funeral" and "delight and dole." His words well express the theme of the first part of this scene. The gravediggers are identified as "two clowns;" that is, they are lowly characters who provide broad comedy in the midst of tragic action. It should be apparent that the comic element in this scene is significant. Moreover, the first gravedigger, so far as his gift for paradox is concerned, has at his level a certain affinity with Hamlet himself when the prince chooses to exercise his sardonic wit. However brief his appearance may be in this play, the first gravedigger is a memorable figure.

Incongruity is basic to comedy. For these two lowly gravediggers to discuss with such intensity a profound theological and legal question, and especially to hear the first one introduce into his argument Latin terms and organize his argument in strict accordance with the rules of Aristotelian logic, is a wonderful comedy of words. Instead of *se defendendo* (in self-defense), the first gravedigger says *se offendendo,* and he pronounces the Latin *ergo* (therefore) as *argal.* In what amounts to a burlesque of the scholastic method of argument, he defines the "three branches" of an act, with hilarious results. The two are no less amusing when the transition is made to Adam, the first delver and the father of the human race—proof that the gravediggers, like gardeners and ditch-diggers, are descendents of the first human being, who was a gentleman.

Few can miss the underlying seriousness in much of this comedy. It serves to emphasize the Christian framework of *Hamlet* and to remind one that Hamlet himself is a Christian prince who has been called upon to carry out revenge. Ophelia's guilt, if any, depends upon whether or not her drowning was a voluntary act. If it was voluntary, obviously she was guilty of self-murder. Other lives have been taken in the course of the action, including that of Polonius; others soon will be lost—and not just the life of Claudius. The prince has been, and will be, involved in most of these deaths. What is the extent of his guilt? In all instances does he, and will he, function as the righteous minister of God's justice or as a scourge?

The gravediggers' dialogue, with its emphasis largely on death, also serves as a prologue to the "worm's meat" or "Dance of Death" theme developed in this same scene by Hamlet. Perhaps there is even relevance in the song which the first gravedigger sings, a conventional Tudor one in which youth and age are contrasted. But youth and age are not the only subjects of the song; love and the denial of love are also contrasted. Time is the destroyer of youth, inevitably; but it can also destroy love. And this too looks forward to the subject of Hamlet's morbid remarks.

When Hamlet sees the first gravedigger toss up the skulls, he exclaims: "How the knave jowls it to the ground, as if it were Cain's jawbone, that did the first murder!" Since Cain's crime was fratricide, the importance of this exclamation is evident. One recalls Claudius' words, spoken in soliloquy, after the Mouse-trap had been sprung:

O, my offence is rank, it smells to heaven;
It hath the primal eldest curse upon't,
A brother's murder.

(Act III, Sc. 3, 36-38)

Carried along by his imagination, Hamlet meditates on the ironical fact that overreaching politicians, lawyers with all their tricks, self-seeking courtiers, vain court ladies, even those held to be models of greatness in this world ultimately are no more than the "quintessence of dust." Among the examples of earthly vanity which he cites, the following is the culminating one:

Now get you to my lady's chamber, and tell
her, let her paint an inch thick, to this favor she must come.
Make her laugh at that.

(Act V, Sc. 1, 180-83)

It is quite possible that more than human vanity is involved here. In two significant earlier passages, comparable references to woman's efforts at beautification were used to show hypocrisy or dishonesty in general. The first was included in the king's aside after he heard Polonius instruct Ophelia on how to conduct herself once she was "loosed" upon Hamlet; the second reference was part of Hamlet's bitter words to Ophelia in the nunnery scene. The conclusion to be drawn, then, is that Hamlet's meditations are not just another example of morbid preoccupation with death, amounting to what some insist is a death wish, nor a vision of his own impending death. Rather, they underscore once more, and this late in the play, the extent of his disillusionment. Had he swept to his revenge and survived to rule Denmark, Hamlet's outlook on life could never be the optimistic one which once made it possible for him to embrace the idealistic Renaissance view of man as the paragon of animals.

The discussion of Ophelia's burial, in which the priest and Laertes take part, calls for some commentary. The priest's insistence that "Her death was doubtful" is at variance with Gertrude's report of accidental death in the preceding scene. One learns that Ophelia is to be buried in sanctified ground only because "great command o'ersways the order," an indication that the king himself interceded after the coroner's verdict. It is established, however, that Ophelia died chaste and therefore is allowed "virgin rites." Not without interest also is the fact that once more she is associated with flowers. "Lay her i' th' earth," Laertes exclaims in anguish, "And from her fair and unpolluted flesh/May violets spring!" Gertrude, who appears most sympathetic in this scene, scatters flowers on the coffin and says, "Sweets to the sweet! Farewell!" When Ophelia first appeared in this play she was associated with flowers and specifically with the violet, a symbol of faithfulness, but also a flower which is "sweet, not lasting;" she was associated also with other "infants of the spring." Much later in the play, a demented Ophelia distributed flowers among the members of the court group, but these did not include violets, for they had withered when her father died. All this adds up to an obvious conclusion: Ophelia metaphorically is the flower destroyed by "Contagious blastments," to use Laertes' words, in a Denmark ruled by a corrupt king.

It may come as something of a surprise to find the queen saying, as she scatters flowers on Ophelia's coffin,

> I hoped thou shouldst have been my Hamlet's wife.
> I thought thy bride-bed to have decked, sweet maid,
> And not have strew'd thy grave.
>
> (Act V, Sc. 1, 231-33)

One recalls that both Laertes and Polonius rejected the idea that Hamlet might marry Ophelia, the former arguing that the prince would have to have a political marriage, the latter, typically refusing to believe that Hamlet could have honorable intentions. The queen's words make the death of Ophelia more pathetic. Those who read into *Hamlet* romantic love as the primary element make much of Gertrude's words, just as they do Hamlet's declaration that he loved Ophelia more than forty thousand times as much as brother could love sister.

Overlapping the problem of interpretation here and adding to the complexity are the performances of Laertes and Hamlet. As the funeral procession arrives, the prince speaks of Laertes to Horatio: "That is Laertes, a very noble youth," an unintentionally ironic remark in view of what has been revealed about Laertes. One hardly equates nobility with the kind of underhanded scheming revealed in the last scene of Act IV. It is possible that Hamlet's gracious tribute is intended as a hint for evaluating Laertes' words and actions which soon follow.

Laertes invites great sympathy, just as he did when he and his sister said their farewells early in the play. But, it has been argued, his advice to Ophelia in that early scene was notable for its affected style; it was anything but natural and spontaneous. Consider also the Laertes whose rebellion had, in Claudius' words, looked so "giant-like" and who was willing to "dare damnation," even if he had to slit an adversary's throat in the church. In the present scene, his rhetorical outburst, followed by his leap into the grave, is so excessive that he appears to be overacting the role of the grief-stricken brother, his expression of grief exceeding that of Hecuba, as described in the player's lines from *Aeneas and Dido*. If this is true, then Hamlet's violent reaction is completely understandable, and especially so when one recalls how he had urged the players to avoid overacting and "to hold . . . the mirror up to nature." The prince's own words provide the soundest criticism of Laertes' performance:

> What is he whose grief
> Bears such an emphasis? whose phrase of sorrow
> Conjures the wand'ring stars, and makes them stand
> Like wonder-wounded hearers?
> (Act V, Sc. 1, 241-44)

"This is I,/Hamlet, the Dane!" the prince exclaims when he emerges from where he has been observing what takes place. In these words he takes on his father's title. Is he now a prince who, after indulging himself in meditations or excessive grief, speaks with an absolute authority which indicates that he will no longer procrastinate? Perhaps his experience on the voyage to England and the shock of learning that Ophelia is dead have effected this change in his character. Certainly Hamlet no longer is willing to tolerate "seeming" and "acting," any more than he was willing to tolerate the actions of Rosencrantz and Guildenstern, the king's agents. When Laertes grasps him by the throat, he speaks words which are at once decisive and controlled:

I prithee take thy fingers from my throat,
For, though I am not splentive [hot-tempered] and rash,
Yet have I in me something dangerous,
Which let thy wisdom fear. Hold off thy hand.
(Act V, Sc. 1, 247-50)

ACT V • SCENE 2

Summary

Hamlet now has the time and the opportunity to tell Horatio all that he experienced since he left with Rosencrantz and Guildenstern for England. During the first night at sea, he sought out the quarters occupied by the king's agents, and took the sealed packet containing Claudius' instructions to the English king. Thus he discovered that Claudius had ordered that he be beheaded. Immediately Hamlet devised new instructions in the official style requesting that Claudius' servants who brought the communication to the king of England be put to death. The prince folded these instructions, placed them in the packet, which he sealed, making use of his father's signet. Then he replaced the packet. On the next day, the sea-fight with the pirates took place, as Hamlet informed Horatio in his letter. Only Hamlet was taken captive; the others proceeded on the voyage to England.

Horatio is shocked to learn the extent of Claudius' villainy. Horatio points out that Claudius will soon learn what has happened to Rosencrantz and Guildenstern, but Hamlet replies that he is safe for the present.

Osric, a messenger from the king, enters. Hamlet promptly recognizes him as the affected, overly polite courtier in the service of Claudius. The prince adopts the same stilted speech employed by this "waterfly" and, with a straight face, asks questions and makes comments intended to make Osric exhaust himself in artificial expression. But at last the message is conveyed: Hamlet is challenged to a friendly duel with Laertes, which is to take place before the king and queen and their attendants. Osric informs the prince that Claudius is confident that he will excel Laertes in swordsmanship. Hamlet declares that he will win for the king's sake if he can. Osric departs, leaving Hamlet and Horatio to remark on how ridiculous he is. Another messager, this time a lord, arrives to ask when Hamlet will be ready for the match. The prince replies that he awaits the king's pleasure. He is told that both king and queen are now coming to witness the contest.

When the two are alone, Horatio warns Hamlet that he will lose the wager, but Hamlet replies that he does not think so, explaining that he has been in continual practice from the time Laertes left for France. Horatio urges him to postpone the match if he has any misgivings and offers to report that the prince is indisposed. But Hamlet is determined; he expresses his willingness to accept whatever is in store for him.

The king, the queen, Laertes, Osric, and various attendants enter. Next to Claudius' chair is a table on which are cups of wine. Before taking his seat, the king puts Laertes' hand into that of Hamlet. Hamlet asks Laertes' pardon for having wronged him, stating that he had not intended any real harm. Laertes replies stiffly that he bears no grudge against Hamlet as far as his personal feelings are concerned, but that he cannot accept the apology until experts in the matter of honor have proved to him that his reputation remains undamaged. Graciously, Hamlet accepts these conditions, and asks that the foils be produced. Laertes is sure that the prince is mocking him, despite Hamlet's denial.

At Claudius' command, Osric brings the foils. While Laertes carefully chooses his, the king asks Hamlet if he knows about the wager. The prince replies that Claudius is wagering on the weaker side, but the king assures him that he knows better, although the odds favor Laertes. Hamlet takes his foil, asking only whether or not it is the same length as the others. Before the contest starts, the king orders that, if Hamlet achieves the first or second hit, cannons will be fired in his honor and the king himself will drink "to Hamlet's better breath." Moreover, he will place a precious pearl in the cup, which will belong to the duelist when he drinks to his own success. After the sound of kettledrums, trumpets, and the blast of cannons, Claudius drinks to Hamlet's health. The match begins.

Hamlet gets the first hit, and Claudius calls for the cup of wine, urging the prince to drink and get the pearl he has won. But Hamlet wishes to continue the contest before drinking. Again he scores a hit, which is acknowledged by Laertes. During the short interval, Claudius remarks to Gertrude that their son will win. Gertrude expresses some doubt, remarking that Hamlet is out of condition. To the distress of Claudius, she picks up the poisoned cup of wine which her husband has prepared for the prince and drinks from it. She then offers it to Hamlet, who again refuses to drink. She offers to wipe his face. This brief interlude provides Laertes with the opportunity to reassure Claudius, but the king is no longer confident that Laertes will be able to score a hit upon Hamlet. Laertes himself, as his aside indicates, is struck at least momentarily with a sense of guilt.

The match is resumed. Laertes does wound Hamlet and in the scuffle between the two, the rapiers are exchanged. After they are parted, Hamlet is able to wound Laertes. At that very moment the queen collapses. Horatio expresses his concern for the bleeding Hamlet, as Osric does for the bleeding Laertes. Laertes, aware that he is close to death, acknowledges that he is "justly kill'd with [his] own treachery." When Hamlet cries out in concern for the queen, Claudius replies that she has fainted at the sight of blood. But Gertrude survives just long enough to tell what has happened: "The drink, the drink! I am poison'd."

Hamlet calls for the doors to be locked and demands that the treachery be exposed to the assembled members of the court. Laertes then speaks up. He states that not only he, but also Hamlet, is near death and that the prince now holds the "treacherous instrument" in his hand. Further, he declares that Gertrude has been poisoned and that the author of all this destruction is Claudius: "The king, the king's to blame." Hamlet lunges at Claudius, exclaiming, "Then, venom, to thy work." The king survives only long enough to hear himself called by his nephew the "incestuous, murd'rous, damned Dane." Before dying, Laertes expresses his conviction that Claudius "is justly serv'd." He asks Hamlet's pardon, assuring the prince that he is not to blame for the deaths of Polonius and Ophelia, and says that he himself is not to be blamed for Hamlet's death.

Hamlet voices his wish that divine justice will rid Laertes of any guilt and adds that he will follow Laertes in death. Turning to his dead mother, he bids the "wretched queen" farewell. He then requests Horatio to report all that happened fully and accurately so that there will be no misunderstandings after his death. But the faithful Horatio is ready to join Hamlet in death and is restrained only by the prince's insistence that he survive to clear Hamlet's "wounded name."

The sounds of marching soldiers and a cannon shot are heard. Osric announces that young Fortinbras, fresh from conquest in Poland, has fired a salute in honor of the newly arrived English ambassadors. Hamlet lives just long enough to prophesy and to approve the election of Fortinbras as king of Denmark. Horatio speaks moving words of sorrow and tribute as Hamlet dies.

Fortinbras and the English ambassadors enter. The Norwegian prince, used to bloodshed in battle, is shocked at the spectacle of death. The ambassadors, gazing on the "dismal" sight, are aware that the news which they were to bring to Claudius has arrived too late: they were to inform him that Rosencrantz and Guildenstern had been executed in accordance with his instructions. Horatio then speaks lines which summarize the whole tragedy.

Fortinbras orders four captains to see to it that Hamlet is accorded full honors, including "soldiers' music and the rites of war."

Commentary

As he begins to fill in the details of what happened to him since he left Denmark, Hamlet admits that "there was a kind of fighting" in his heart. But clearly his inner turmoil has been apparent from the time of his first appearance in this play. Now one is to hear no more expression of self-reproach or doubts that he will act positively against Claudius. What is impressive is his decisiveness. Thanks to what he calls "rashness" and "indiscretion," he is able to formulate a plan and to execute it without delay. As Samuel Johnson observed, Hamlet has found man's wisdom, or reason, to have its limitations: fortune, accident, chance—call it what one will—can determine the course of events, as his own experience aboard the ship proves. He was able to find the commission for his own death; by chance, he had in his possession his father's signet for sealing the forged document. Also by chance, the pirates proved "kind" and they returned him to Denmark.

Of some significance in this scene is Hamlet's summary of Claudius' major offenses:

> He that hath killed my king, and whored my mother,
> Popped in between th' election and my hopes,
> Thrown out his angle for my proper life, . . .
>
> (Act V, Sc. 2, 64-66)

First, there is no evidence of a fixation on an incestuous mother here, perhaps to the disappointment of the neo-Freudians. Second, although Hamlet has made reference to having an ambition to rule Denmark, the protagonist's ambition has not been emphasized before this. Now he accuses his uncle of frustrating that ambition. Coming this late, however, the effect is not to turn the play into an ambition tragedy. Claudius, however formidable as the antagonist to Hamlet, has been identified as a man inferior to the late king. If Hamlet is to perform a public duty in killing Claudius, would it not be his duty also to prove himself to be his father's son by accepting the responsibilities of kingship? In experience, the young prince has grown in stature since he spoke the lines of his first soliloquy and referred to both Claudius and himself in these words: "My father's brother, but no more like my father/Than I to Hercules." He knows that he remains a mortal, but he knows also that he would not be "a king of shreds and patches."

When Horatio reminds Hamlet that Claudius is sure to learn soon what has happened to Rosencrantz and Guildenstern, Hamlet's reply shows him to be controlled and confident. Now he expresses regret that he had so "forgot" himself as to offend Laertes, stating that he sees the image of his own anger in that of Ophelia's brother. Hamlet makes reference here to the fact that both have endured great losses. The prince's determination to win back the good will of Laertes makes understandable his prompt agreement to participate in the fencing match.

Osric, a young courtier, brings to Hamlet the message from Claudius relating to the duel. A few lines would have sufficed for this purpose, but Shakespeare chose to present a full-length portrait of the fashionable, affected courtier, a familiar object of satire during the

Renaissance. Hamlet identifies him as a "water-fly"—that is, an insect darting about the surface of water without any apparent purpose. Such lines as Hamlet's "Put your bonnet to his right use. 'Tis for the head" tell the reader how excessively formal Osric's gestures are. The courtier's style of speech, burlesqued by the prince, is marked by an overuse of Latinisms and elaborate metaphors. The attention which Shakespeare pays to Osric may be justified, at least to some extent, on the grounds that he serves to illustrate artificiality and pretense which characterize the court, the leader of which is Claudius. But since both qualities have been well established already, some may conclude that the portrait of Osric is unnecessary.

"You will lose this wager, my lord," says Horatio after Osric has left. But Hamlet reassures his friend, saying that, while Laertes was in France, he (Hamlet) has "been in continual practice." Later in the present scene, Gertrude will remark that her son is out of condition. Yet there is no question of Hamlet's skill as a swordsman. Ophelia's tribute described Hamlet as the ideal prince and courtier—the accomplished Renaissance man, "The courtier's, soldier's, scholar's, eye, tongue, sword."

When Horatio urges him to consider withdrawing from the match, Hamlet makes a meaningful reply:

> . . . we defy augury. There's a
> special providence in the fall of a sparrow. If it be now, 'tis
> not to come; if it be not to come, it will be now; if it be not
> now, yet it will come. The readiness is all.
>
> (Act V, Sc. 2, 208-211)

What the prince says here is consistent with what he said earlier in this scene when he declared that "There's a divinity that shapes our ends." And if he is still heartsick, this passage provides additional evidence that no longer is there "a kind of fighting" in his heart—the kind that, early in the play, made him lament the fact that he was called upon to act violently because the "time is out of joint." Hamlet now seems to have resolved all doubts as to whether he functions as minister or as scourge. Finally, he no longer fears death or what may await him after death. When he says, "There's a special providence in the fall of a sparrow," he is, of course, paraphrasing verses from the Bible—Matthew 10:28-31; Luke 12:4-7.

The "readiness is all." This dictum suggests that Hamlet has mastered passion. Inevitably it calls to mind his praise of Horatio as a man who is not passion's slave. In *King Lear,* Edgar, striving once more to win over his blind and oppressed father, the Earl of Gloucester, from despair, said:

What, in ill thoughts again? Men must endure

Their going hence, even as their coming hither;
Ripeness is all.

(Act V, Sc. 2, 9-11)

Gloucester, like Hamlet, would have welcomed death, although, unlike Hamlet, he was not restrained by conscience. He had lost faith in a supreme power or powers concerned with man's destiny. Thanks to the good offices of his son Edgar, he finally learns to accept fortune's blows with patience. Hamlet, who now knows that "readiness is all," has also come to terms with fortune.

In his apology to Laertes, Hamlet shows graciousness and sincerity. One remembers how he told Horatio how much he regretted his behavior in the graveyard. Nevertheless, there are certain disturbing elements in this episode before the fencing match. He tells Laertes that "madness" has been his enemy, yet again and again, from the time he told Horatio and members of the guard that he planned to adopt an "antic disposition," evidence has been presented to show that, however extravagant his words, and actions may have been on occasion, he was anything but demented. The conclusion to be made is that he refers here to that "kind of fighting" in his heart which led to emotional extremes. Ironically, if Gertrude spoke truly when she said that she had hoped that Ophelia would have become Hamlet's wife, Laertes might have become the prince's brother. "I'll be your foil," says Hamlet in the spirit of good fellowship, punning upon the word, which may mean "rapier" or "something which, by contrast, enhances a jewel." But, as things turn out, *Laertes* is the foil—in a far different sense.

No one is likely to underestimate the king as he appears during these preliminaries. From his first appearance in this play, he has demonstrated his skill at pretense. It is he who places Laertes' hand in that of Hamlet; all hear him express absolute confidence in, and support of, his nephew. With an apparent abundance of good will, he promises Hamlet a princely reward. At his orders, music is played, and he drinks to Hamlet's success. Claudius is no ordinary villain; he is an accomplished one, the mighty opposite of the tragic hero. If Laertes were to wound Hamlet and survive unscathed, he alone would be aware of Claudius' fear and hatred of Hamlet.

Queen Gertrude is heard from only after the match has begun and Hamlet has scored the first hit with his blunted foil. No one should misinterpret her remark "He's fat, and scant of breath," made just before she offers to wipe Hamlet's brow and prepares to drink to his success. Yet a few have managed to do just that, concluding that the prince is overweight. But, as King James I is reported to have said, no melancholy man was ever fat. The context should tell even a modern critic that Gertrude is referring to the fact that Hamlet is perspiring, perhaps excessively—an indication, as she believes, that he is out of condition.

The action that follows is as exciting as any to be found in drama. Laertes is allowed to express twinges of conscience just before he wounds Hamlet; and, when he himself is fatally wounded, he has the good grace to acknowledge that his own treachery is responsible for his impending death. Moreover, just after the queen cries out that she has been poisoned, he survives to place the blame upon Claudius. Demands of the plot at this point, in part, explain Laertes' free confession and accusation. But it is not inappropriate that Laertes, who shortly before had declared that he stood aloof from Hamlet "in terms of honor" and then faced the prince armed with an unblunted and poisoned rapier, should be allowed to redeem himself through full confession. Claudius must, and does, remain the villain of the piece.

"The point envenomed too?" exclaims Hamlet at the moment of complete discovery, aware that he will soon join his mother and Laertes in death. One recalls that venom—poison—used by Claudius was the source of the rottenness in Denmark. It has spread throughout Elsinore and beyond. Polonius, Ophelia, and Rosencrantz and Guildenstern are among its victims.

At long last, Hamlet slays Claudius. The prince survives not only to philosophize briefly on "this fell sergeant, Death," who is so "strict in his arrest," but also to request Horatio to clear his "wounded name." Certainly he does not want subjects of the crown to believe that his killing of Claudius was the last and most shocking action of a Hamlet who, in the words of the first gravedigger, was mad. Even less does he want to be remembered as the Pyrrhus-type of king-killer. Hamlet's concept of honor, implicit from the beginning, is something far above that held by Laertes and Polonius. He wishes to be remembered as the worthy son of the superior King Hamlet. The moving words of Horatio, who knew him best, provide the most truthful and sincere epitaph:

Now cracks a noble heart. Good-night, sweet prince,
And flights of angels sing thee to thy rest.

(Act V, Sc. 2, 348-49)

Hamlet was the "sweet prince"; and, in the Renaissance, the word *sweet* (like the adjective *gentle*) had special force, emphasizing superiority when applied to a person.

Fortinbras, who arrives near the very end of the play, also provides an epitaph:

Let four captains
Bear Hamlet like a soldier to the stage,
For he was likely, had he been put on,
To have prov'd most royal, . . .

(Act V, Sc. 2, 385-87)

It is quite significant that Hamlet, who did not survive to rule Denmark (and in that sense had not "been put on"), is accorded a soldier's funeral. One is reminded again that the issue in the conflict between Hamlet and Claudius was a public one involving the health of the state.

In his dying words, Hamlet casts his vote for Fortinbras as the new ruler of Denmark. Fortinbras, has been presented as one of the foils to Hamlet. Some critics are sure that his ascension to the throne is especially fitting, since Hamlet has paid the price for his inability to master passion before it was too late for him to avoid catastrophe (which in Renaissance high tragedy is always the death of the protagonist). Others, conceding that Hamlet failed in that he did not survive to prove himself his father's son as ruler of Denmark, insist that the very condition which made inevitable his failure, especially his unwillingness to act without much thought, is the measure of his greatness. For them, the prince emerges finally as the sacrificial victim, one whose death is inevitable but which makes possible the purging of great evil and the restoration of a moral universe.

Characters

Methods of Analyzing Characters

1. Describing the Characters

It is always a good idea to begin any commentary on characters with a brief description of each of them—what they are like, what they seem to think about themselves, etc. This kind of brief survey of the characters assures the student that he will not assume too much when discussing the characters in more complex or sophisticated ways. It also forces the student not to overlook any of the various characters' essential attributes. It should be pointed out that Hamlet is the young prince of Denmark, or that Othello is a Moor; then these simple facts should be amplified by whatever else we know. All in all, then, one should make a short survey of the characteristics—both emotional and physical—of the characters.

2. Analysis of Character Development

Probably the most important aspect of character analysis is the treatment of the development of the characters, and primarily the main characters. It is all-important to explain how a character *changes* in the course of the play. And one must also explain *why* those changes take place *when* they do. Even if a character seems static throughout, there must be an explanation. It may be that Shakespeare is using the character as a prop, a necessary convenience, or simply as an illustrative example of an alternative to the mode of existence courted by the hero or heroine. When certain emotions—such as greed, hate, love, revenge, bitterness, confidence—come to the surface, we should try to understand precisely how and why. Is there violent reaction or calm acceptance? Does Lady Macbeth's incipient guilt plunge her into a quasi-psychotic depression? The basic changes, not the minor ones, should be briefly delineated and more thoroughly analyzed. Is it right that a certain character feels as he does? Is it human or is it extreme? Abnormal or normal? Unusual or typical? Surprising or expected? Are changes foreshadowed? Are they ever illogical or too contrived? All literary analysis consists of an extended process of asking questions. And this questioning process is particularly vital to the analysis of characters. We must understand why characters behave and change in order to understand the meaning of the entire play. Aside from all the usual reasons that characters change, as, for example, when one's mother or relative is killed and one suddenly is filled with a desire for revenge and acts accordingly, many explanations of character change can be found either in their motivation, as it is developed by the dramatist, or by the demands of the themes. And these will be our next two considerations.

3. Motivation

In considering the motivation of characters we are fundamentally enlarging our answer to the "why" of character behavior. Shakespeare is of course very "modern" in his grasp of human psychology and the ways in which thought should be translated into action. What incites Hamlet's anger at the beginning of the play is his sense of the immorality and haste of his mother's marriage to his uncle so soon after the death of his father. Later, after his encounter with the ghost, Hamlet has an even greater claim to outrage. After learning that his uncle has murdered his father, Hamlet's actions become motivated by revenge. While revenge is the force that drives Hamlet, it is self-preservation that motivates Claudius in his actions. To conceal his guilt and maintain both his kingdom and his queen are Claudius' prime concerns. There are explanations for the behavior of all the characters in the play, and these explanations or motivations must be considered by analyzing who and what they are.

4. Thematic Characters

Often we discover that the behavior of certain characters can be explained by themes. That is, a character like Iago may act in evil ways consistently because allegorically he represents evil. The play is about the destruction wrought by evil and thus Iago may be said to be a "thematic character," less human and less complicated, while more conventional and "stock." Any character in any play may be thought of as a thematic character from one point of view or another, but we generally limit our use of the term to characters who clearly represent certain dominant abstractions which are clashing in a play—i.e., good and evil, love and hatred, loyalty and disloyalty, faithfulness and unfaithfulness (notice how all are extensions of good and evil). Most tragedies involve thematic characters, but not in such ways that we choose to discuss the characters in those terms. In general, it is better to search for what is human or unique about certain characters, but it is always worthwhile to mention briefly the thematic possibilities of the characters. Why are they in the play? Why do they behave as they do? How does their behavior demonstrate particular ideas?

5. Analyzing Character Relationships

Although inherent in the other methods, the analysis of the relationships between the characters can be used as a complete analysis in itself. The world of the play is largely defined by the nature of the different relationships. Hamlet's relationships with the other characters in the play reveal different aspects of his personality and the personalities of those with whom he is in contact. The "more" or the "less" of the basic relationships of friendship, marriage, command, etc., must be clarified, for through this clarification of relationships, we arrive at a greater understanding of the characters themselves.

Character Sketches

Hamlet

Hamlet is the prince of Denmark, son of the late King Hamlet and Queen Gertrude, and nephew of Claudius. He is a young man of physical valor and scholarly preoccupations, and a student at the University of Wittenberg. He has returned home to find his father dead and his mother married to his uncle. He is in a distracted state of mourning, and even more significantly perhaps, of grief over his mother's quick remarriage. His father's ghost appears, tells of his murder at the hand of Claudius, and urges Hamlet to avenge both the foul play and the "incestuous" marriage.

Many penetrating and scholarly studies have been written evaluating Hamlet, and his profoundly searching soliloquies have been exhaustively analyzed. Most authorities agree that Hamlet is an exceedingly complex individual who, though gifted with the sword, is given more to philosophizing than to direct action. Hamlet does not view the world, himself, or even the villain of this play in a simple detached manner; he studies and restudies the behavior of his fellow men, as well as his own behavior. His many soliloquies on his procrastination in executing the command of his father's ghost ("To be or not to be" is the most renowned) testify to his failure to come to terms with his inner being. While he accumulates more and more evidence of Claudius' obvious guilt, he constantly returns to the theme of his mother's remarriage—a source of pain equally as unbearable as the circumstances of his father's death. It is ironic that the one time Hamlet acts decisively without some meditation, he kills Polonius, mistakenly thinking him to be the king. When Hamlet does at last kill Claudius, he himself is dying, and he is spontaneously provoked by Gertrude's death and Laertes' accusation.

Hamlet is a man of integrity, obviously honored and beloved by his people, but he sacrifices even Ophelia to his overwhelming preoccupation with Claudius and Gertrude. The more Hamlet becomes obsessed with the deed he knows he must do, the less he is able to execute it. Hamlet is a truly heroic figure, but his need to dwell on his tragic situation, led to his own death.

Claudius

Claudius, the king, has murdered his brother, Hamlet's father, and married Queen Gertrude. Claudius is contrasted with Hamlet as a man of action. If evil is essential to the realization of a goal, then Claudius will sacrifice the ethic for the end. He does not commit evil carelessly, but is quite ready to waive morality in the light of necessity. He is strong-minded, passionate, and above all, directional. He makes his plans and proceeds accordingly. He is intelligent in his understanding of human motivation, and knows how to manipulate those around him. He is fully aware of Hamlet's suspicions and the motive behind Hamlet's supposed madness. Only twice, once in an aside to Polonius' description of Ophelia, and more forcibly in the scene where he is praying, does Claudius verbalize any qualms of conscience, and even here, the thoughts are not allowed to interfere with the resolution. Claudius is astute and calculating, ambitious and ruthless in his pursuit of power. These traits, in combination with Hamlet's apparent uncertainty, delay his death until Laertes' accusation in the final scene of the play.

Gertrude

Gertrude, queen of Denmark, wife of Claudius and mother of Hamlet, is innocent of the murder of her husband, Hamlet's father. She obviously loved and was loved and revered by her first husband. But the combination of her own meekness and the strength of Claudius' passion and power to act have led her to this second marriage. She had questioned neither her husband's untimely death nor her hasty remarriage, accepting both as natural to the order of things, until Hamlet's return to Denmark. Now she is "cleft . . . in twain," torn between her love for her son Hamlet and her allegiance to her husband and King, Claudius. Hamlet plants in her a guilt she did not feel; she is tormented by both her divided loyalties of the present, and her sudden conscious recognition of the immorality of her remarriage. Unable to do more than show anguish at a pain new to the hitherto evenness of her life, Gertrude allows Claudius to plan their joint treatment of Hamlet: their attitudes toward his madness, the trip to England, the duel with Laertes. In all these events she is outside the planned treachery, yet she unwittingly conforms to Claudius' schemings, and in the end, dies a victim of the poisoned drink intended for Hamlet.

Ophelia

Ophelia, daughter of Polonius and Laertes' sister, embodies the romantic notion of womanhood: she is beautiful, sweet, industrious, gentle. She loves Hamlet, and initially, believes in his love for her. But when her brother and father lecture her on the impossibility of this love and her foolishness, she bows to their authority and withdraws. Hamlet's "madness" first confuses her; then it wounds and terrifies her. Although she reveals an intelligence in her conversations with Laertes and Polonius, and in her behavior at "the play," she is completely unable to comprehend the treachery of the court and the complex behavior of Hamlet. Direct, honest, and trusting, the deceitful intrigues which surround her, combined with the sudden death of her beloved father, throw her into a state of madness. Ophelia's drowning, described by the queen as an accident resulting from her distraught behavior, is sometimes thought to have been the suicide of an innocent, unworldly maiden who can no longer cope with the complexity of her life. There is little factual proof for this latter interpretation of her death though.

Polonius

Polonius, father of Laertes and Ophelia, is the lord chamberlain in the court of Claudius. Although not an evil man, Polonius is nevertheless cynical and self-seeking in his eagerness to receive the favor of the king and queen. Pragmatic and realistic, he gives his departing son advice calculated to make Laertes a friend of everyone and offensive to none. In like manner, he instructs Ophelia to ignore the attentions of a man placed as highly as Hamlet. He is convinced that the prince, above Ophelia socially, is only selfishly motivated. Polonius' craving to be esteemed by the king and queen, coupled with his limited sensitivity, leads him to verbosity and clumsy meddling. In an attempt to ingratiate himself, he offers to spy upon the interview between the queen and Hamlet. Startled by what he takes to be the queen's cry for help, he reveals his presence to Hamlet, who, believing the king to be thus hidden, draws his sword and kills Polonius through the curtains.

Laertes

Laertes, Polonius' son and brother of Ophelia, is somewhat cynical like his father in advising Ophelia of the impossibility of love with Prince Hamlet. But Laertes has a basic courage and honesty. If he is rash and hot-headed, it is because he takes it upon himself to avenge first his father's death, and then his sister's insanity. He seems to have had a youthful fling in Paris, but he returns to Denmark to the serious responsibility of manhood—that is, to uncover his father's murderer and to avenge Polonius' almost-secret, unhonored burial. While his wrath leads him to use an unprotected and poisoned foil in his duel with Hamlet, he is more Claudius' dupe than his co-conspirator. His conscience troubles him during the exchange, and when he falls victim as a result of a confusion of weapons, he confesses his treachery to Hamlet, and dies indicting the king.

Horatio

Horatio, a young Dane and friend of Hamlet, has been away at the University of Wittenberg and has returned for the funeral of Hamlet's father. His is a most sympathetic portrait: a man who is both a scholar and a person of irrefutable good character. Although there is always recognition of Hamlet's princely status, Horatio is treated as a true friend by the prince and becomes his confidant. He is drawn as a learned man, of even disposition, truly just and honorable without being falsely moved by passion. It is Horatio who first informs Hamlet of the appearance of his father's ghost. The prince later confides to Horatio the bloody deeds of his uncle, his grief over the queen's marriage, the treachery of Rosencrantz and Guildenstern, and his plan to observe Claudius at "the play." Concerned for the safety of his friend, Horatio tries to dissuade Hamlet from dueling with Laertes, and in his selfless loyalty, wants to drink the poison as Hamlet is dying. The prince restrains him, and Horatio remains to tell Fortinbras and all the world of the tragedies which have occurred.

Rosencrantz and Guildenstern

Two contemporaries of Hamlet, and companions of his youth, they are recalled to Denmark by Claudius and act as his willing tools. Their feigned friendship with Hamlet, which the prince knows to be false, is typical of their servile behavior in deference to social rank. Hamlet likens them to a "sponge," which absorbs the orders and rewards of the King and eventually, is squeezed dry into nothingness. Hamlet uncovers their deceitfulness and ironically arranges for their deaths in place of his—a just reward for their disloyalty.

Fortinbras

Fortinbras, prince of Norway, has embarked upon a military venture, designed to regain for his country the lands forfeited by his father in combat with Hamlet's father. He is dissuaded from this enterprise by Claudius' warning to his old uncle in Norway, who restrains Fortinbras and sets him upon a different course of attack. At the close of the play, Fortinbras reveals admiration for Hamlet's princely qualities, and sorrow for the tragic deaths about him. Nonetheless, he makes it quite clear that he will assert his right of ascendancy to the now-empty throne.

Osric

He is a young courtier who carries Claudius' message to Hamlet, proposing the duel between Hamlet and Laertes. Osric has the outwardly verbose and superficial manner of the courtier. Hamlet mocks him in their interchange, but Osric is insensitive to the intended ridicule.

Questions and Answers on the Characters

Question 1.

From the play, quoting where you can, show Hamlet to be excitable, affectionate, melancholic, sarcastic and refined.

Answer

EXCITABLE: When the ghost appears to him, his fate cries out:

And makes each pretty artery in this body
As hardy as the Nemean lion's nerve.

The ghost finds him "apt," and indeed, at that moment, when "desperate with imagination," he longed to sweep to his revenge "With wings as swift/As meditation or the thoughts of love."

He was still under the influence of excitement produced by his interview with the ghost when he decided to assume the role of a madman.

After the trial of the play, in "the very witching time of night," he could:

drink hot blood,
And do such bitter business as the day
Would quake to look on.

In such a mood, he cruelly abused his mother and murdered Polonius, mistaking him for the king. At other times his excitable nature was roused to passion by the player's speech, by the example of Fortinbras, and by the sight of Laertes' boisterous grief at Ophelia's grave. On this last occasion he falls into uncontrollable rage:

Woo't weep? woo't fight? woo't fast? woo't tear thyself?
Woo't drink up essil? eat a crocodile
I'll do't,

he exclaims, and his actions show that the violence of his emotion has in it something dangerous that wisdom may well fear. But his passion was as short-lived as it was violent. To Horatio he repented, and promised to make amends to Laertes when the opportunity should arise. All his sudden actions (the dooming to death of his schoolfellows, the murder of the king, the snatching of the bowl of poison from Horatio), were performed on impulse and in sudden inspirations of excited feeling.

AFFECTIONATE: He respected, admired, and loved his father, whom he describes as his "dear murthered father," and of whom he says:

'A was a man, take him for all in all,
I shall not look upon his like again.

Hamlet had loved Ophelia tenderly and she responded with gentle, clinging affection. At her graveside, in passionate words, he exclaims:

Forty thousand brothers
Could not with all their quantity of love
Make up my sum.

But his affection for Horatio was more deep-seated. In his chosen friend's nature he found something that made up for his own over-sensitivity. In him he found relief from his sense of loneliness. He shows his affection for Horatio by saying of him:

Since my dear soul was mistress of my choice,
And could of men distinguish, her election
Hath sealed thee for herself.

Hamlet's gentle nature feels an affectionate sympathy even for Laertes in his grief; he "freely embraces his offered love like love, and by the image of his own cause sees the portraiture of his."

MELANCHOLIC: He first appears in the drama dressed in solemn mourning, with "dejected 'haviour of the visage," the clouds still hanging on him. The queen urges him:

Do not for ever with thy veiled lids
Seek for thy noble father in the dust.

In his first soliloquy he utters the despondent words:

O that this too, too sullied flesh would melt,
Thaw, and resolve itself into a dew!

He regards the world as a prison, the earth "an unweeded garden," "a sterile promontory," the heavens as "a foul and pestilent congregation of vapours". He loses all his humor and "walks for hours together'' in the palace hall, his general behavior the picture of melancholy. "Look where sadly the poor wretch comes reading," said the queen on one occasion. After the player's recitation he refers to his own melancholy mood, and considers the possibility that he may have been all along the dupe of the devil, who:

> Out of my weakness and my melancholy,
> As he is very potent with such spirits,
> Abuses me to damn me.

He seems to revel in thoughts of death and suicide, and from his interview with Ophelia, the king concludes that:

> There's something in his soul
> O'er which his melancholy sits on brood.

All his fits of impulsive action are followed by periods of melancholy and despair. After his first interview with the ghost, he cursed his fate; after the death of Polonius, he wept; after his passionate scene with Laertes, his silence did "sit, drooping." In the last act, his conversation with Laertes, and the solemn reflections which fall from his lips in the graveyard scene, show the melancholy cast of thought that had now become habitual with him.

SARCASTIC: Many sarcastic images, comparisons, and allusions escape from Hamlet in his varying moods. At times his sarcasm is witty and humorous, as when he fools Polonius (Act II, Sc. 2; Act III, Sc. 2), or ridicules the courtiers (Act II, Sc. 2; Act IV, Sc. 2); when he indulges in trifling conversation with Ophelia (Act III, Sc. 2). At other times he expresses himself with bitter sarcasm, showing his undisguised contempt for the hypocrisy, deceit, and shallowness with which he is surrounded. He speaks of the king in terms of scornful disgust: he is "a vice of kings," "a villain and a cutpurse," "a king of shreds and patches," a "thing of nothing," who delights in revels and in drunkenness.

During the interlude, and in the presence of the king, Hamlet seems to find some compensation for his inaction in sarcastic utterances:

> 'Tis a knavish piece of work; but what o' that? Your Majesty,
> and we that have free souls, it touches us not; let the galled
> jade wince, our withers are unwrung.

Even the queen, his mother, is not spared, although once he dearly loved her; now, he treats her with contempt. With cruel irony he addresses her:

For who that's but a queen, fair, sober, wise,
Would from a paddock, from a bat, a gib,
Such dear concernings hide?

On the point of leaving for England, he sarcastically takes leave of his father with the words, "Farewell, dear mother;" and in the grave-yard scene, his aversion to all that is false or affected is shown by his sarcastic and ironical allusions to politicians, courtiers, and lawyers. Pointing to the skull he holds in his hand, he says:

Now get you to my lady's chamber, and tell her, let her paint an inch thick, to this favour must she come; make her laugh at that.

REFINED: He has no sympathy with the revels and drunkenness of his age (Act I, Sc. 4). A man endowed with "noble and most sovereign reason," he associated with scholars and artists. He composed verses, and carried books about with him. He possessed "The courtier's, soldier's, scholar's eye, tongue, sword," and was:

The expectancy and rose of the fair state,
The glass of fashion and the mould of form,
The observed of all observers.

By nature, he preferred meditation and philosophy, and the emotional side of his character was no less highly developed than the intellectual. To the gravedigger he was mad, but to Horatio he was "a noble heart." He was deeply hurt by his mother's lack of shame and modesty, and the king's grossness and lust were more revolting to him than the crime of murder.

Question 2.
How is Polonius viewed by the other major characters in the play?

Answer
Polonius is the adviser of the king, whom he serves to the best of his ability with fidelity and zeal. He possesses a certain amount of the confidence of his royal master, who, however, consults him more often on domestic than on state affairs. As a result of his long experience, he has acquired a considerable share of worldly wisdom, which he is fond of exhibiting on all occasions, whether called for or not. The king thinks of him "as of a man faithful and honorable"; the queen speaks of him as a "good old man." Laertes's love for him is such that, to avenge his death, he "hazards both the worlds," and Ophelia, in her madness, retains none but the sweetest memories of him.
Such is the light in which he was regarded by those whom natural

affection blinded to his defects, or by people who saw in him a means of serving their own ends. Hamlet, however, brought an unbiased judgment to bear upon his character, and that he was not very much mistaken in his unfavorable opinion of the "wretched, rash, intruding fool," will be evident from the following considerations:

(1) Polonius was deceitful and cunning, as is shown by the indirect, crooked methods he adopted for obtaining any information he needed: he hired spies to watch Laertes when he was in Paris; he used his daughter as an instrument for discovering the cause of Hamlet's madness; and he was unscrupulous enough to play the part of a spy himself.

(2) He is suspicious and prying, meddles with everything, listens to slander about his daughter, mistrusts his son, and boasts to the king of his ability to find "where truth is hid, though it were hid, indeed, within the centre."

(3) He is superficial, shallow, conceited, and long-winded, he prides himself on his knowledge and judgment, his literary, critical, and histrionic ability. Yet all the while he is exposing his own folly and ignorance.

(4) He is ignorant of true wisdom, and entirely misunderstands Hamlet's nature and actions. He sins against the canons of good taste even while propounding them. He is, in fact, one of those "seeming wise men," of whom it has been said that they "may make shift to get opinion, but let no man choose them for employment."

Question 3.
Describe the character of Gertrude in terms of her innocence.

Answer
Despite some uncertainty at times, the verdict of Gertrude's complicity in the murder of her first husband and in continued intrigue is "not guilty." Not only has the ghost (proved trustworthy) counseled Hamlet to "leave her to heaven," but we realize her lack of knowledge of Claudius' actions and intentions during the scene with Hamlet in her bedchamber and during the dueling scene. She has been maneuvered by her second husband into moves which aid his cause. The picture of the queen that arises is that of a gullible, somewhat slow-witted, easily manipulated, changeable, and inconstant woman. She has been wooed and won over easily by her husband's brother, perhaps even before his murder (probably through flattery). She avoids self-accusation and analysis, and seems incapable of coming to grips with unpleasantness. She grasps at easy answers and makes excuses for everyone. Therefore, the effect on her of the interview with Hamlet, (Act III, Sc. 4) and of Ophelia's madness and suicide is confusion and bewilderment. In a sense, she ironically balances Ophelia in their mixture of immorality and innocence; or, to look at it differently, the queen is as unsuspicious

at the wrong time as Polonius is suspicious of the wrong circumstances. There is little to admire in Gertrude, regardless of what pardons we make for her.

Question 4.

Briefly describe Rosencrantz and Guildenstern, Osric, and the gravediggers.

Answer

Rosencrantz and Guildenstern are important as representing a type rather than for any actions or utterances of their own. They represent the type of fawning, flattering courtiers that "soak up the king's countenance, his rewards, his authorities," and are ready for any mean and immoral work in his service. Such characters may be supposed to have had a good education—they were Hamlet's school-fellows—and to have been well versed in the arts and accomplishments of a conventional society. They are an indivisible couple, each deriving support and confidence from the presence of the other. Devoid of all originality, they form their opinions on all subjects in accordance with the fashion of the day, being well satisfied if they can only get "the tune of the time and outward habit of encounter." Their knowledge is superficial and their intelligence mediocre, so that they are easily foiled by Hamlet in any argument or combat of wit. They are not of the stuff that great criminals are made, having neither power of initiation, nor courage, nor acuteness of judgment, nor shrewdness. They are fools rather than knaves, and though they meet with a more severe punishment than they deserve, we are conscious of no pity for them.

Osric is a fashionable gentleman of the court. He has much land, and therefore stands high in the king's favor. He is a friend of Laertes, whose qualities he admires, and for whom he acts as second in the duel. His language is affected and pedantic. He deals in high-flown compliments, and makes a great parade of politeness. When his shallowness and superficiality are exposed by Hamlet, he either does not, or will not, perceive that he is the object of Hamlet's satire. There is some doubt as to whether or not he was aware of the treachery against Hamlet's life, but we cannot fail to regard with some suspicion the man who gave the combatants their foils, and to whom Laertes, when wounded with the poisoned point, exclaims:

Why, as a woodcock to mine own springe, Osric,
I am justly killed with mine own treachery.
(Act V, Sc. 2, 295-96)

The gravediggers are introduced as they are discussing the legality of Ophelia's burial in sanctified ground. On this, as on other topics, they express their opinions with almost socialistic freedom. This tendency toward socialism is perceived by Hamlet, who says, "the age is grown so picked that the toe of the peasant comes so near the heel of the courtier, he galls his kibe." These ale-washed wits have lost all feeling of their business, and sing and crack jokes over their dismal work, as though gravedigging were the most pleasant trade on earth. Like other characters in the play, the first clown seeks to show his cleverness and ingenuity in words; he has caught the trick of the age, and can reason and philosophize with the prince of philosophers.

Structure

Methods of Analyzing Structure

For art to exist in any real way, something has to be *made.* A given work of art, therefore, has some sort of definite structure, even if that structure is an abstract kind of formless entity. The structure of literary works of art is not something uniform. From genre to genre, and within each genre, there are virtually countless kinds of structures. It would be idle work to attempt to discuss the structures of *King Lear* and *The Catcher in the Rye* in the same way. The purpose of this section is to familiarize students with some of the ways in which we can discuss structure, with a particular interest in a Shakespearean drama. After introducing several methods of analyzing structure, we will illustrate the ways in which these methods can be used in answering particular questions.

1. Analysis

The first place to start an analysis of structure is in consideration of plot. If plot is, as Aristotle stated, the first principle and soul of tragedy, it seems obvious that we should come to certain conclusions about the plot before passing on to other more sophisticated dimensions. In a certain sense, structure is another word for plot. Both describe what *is*; that is, both direct us to *what happens when,* which is the heart of the drama. The structure, in other words, is the way in which the events of the play are put together. The turning points, reversals, or alterations within the action of the play are all presented in a definite way for a definite purpose. The student's task is to begin by establishing clearly in his mind the *order* of the events and then go on to *explanations* of that order. Most dramatists are, fortunately, logical as well as entertaining. We are not so much called upon to discover their intentions, as rather, the logical reasons for things happening when they do. In short, then, the first way in which to begin an analysis of structure is to delineate and explain the plot in all of its changes and reversals.

2. Synthesis

Whereas in "Analysis" we were concerned with presenting the physical division of the work into its parts, as discovered in the plot, now we should make an effort to explain the development of the connections between the parts. What are the elements which link the various stages of the play? If we are considering a tragedy, how does the dramatist allow the play to flow from preparations for the "fall," through the "fall," and finally into the aftermath? Where are the *key* turning points in the plot? How has the dramatist prepared us in the beginning for what will arrive in the ending? In other words, in synthesis, we attempt to draw all of the parts of the play together. It is one thing to divide the work into its parts, and another to explain the ways in which those parts have been logically connected.

More often than not, the student will find that the *motives of the characters* provide the links between the parts. X happens when it does, because Character Y has certain motives. Particularly in tragedy, we discover the importance of characters' motives in explaining the logic of the plot. Obviously some of the parts of the plot will be joined through contrived "accidents," such as a chance meeting or the discovery of a stolen letter. Since plays are primarily about people, however, more often than not the people in the play become the organizing factors. One character's greed or another one's jealousy will often be sufficient explanation for the fact that everything in the play happens when it does. But whether the student concentrates on character motivation or on the chance events of fortune, he must always be asking whether the structure seems molded in not only a logical but an esthetic way. And this leads us to our next consideration.

3. Esthetic Unity

When the student has divided the work into structural sections, and explained the way in which these sections are held together, he must then decide whether or not the entire framework has esthetic unity. Is the ending artistically derived from the opening? Do the motives of the characters adequately explain their actions? Is there any sort of inconsistency between the characters' motives and actions which the dramatist leaves unexplained? In "Analysis" we divide the action of the play into its logical sections, but now we try to evaluate and to criticize. A good tragedy should have an *introduction, rising action,* a *climax, falling action,* and a *catastrophe.* That is, we need to be introduced to some of the characters, be told about things which have happened recently before the play's opening, and in general given enough information to understand what happens *in* the play.

In the *rising action* are certain events or revealed attitudes which lead logically into the *climax* or chief turning point in the play. There is usually some sort of *exciting action,* something, some reason which sets the rising action in motion. Sometimes it is the challenge to solve a riddle, other times the desire to avenge a slain relative. But there is always some reason which causes the action to commence. After the climax, certain events lead—and usually quite swiftly—to the final catastrophe, which is usually a multiple death or at least the death of the central character. The structure of most classical and Shakespearean tragedy is in accord with this formula and thus keeping these terms in mind often makes it easier to discuss the structure of *any* play, even if there are modifications which must be made.

Whether or not a tragedy moves skilfully through these stages or their explicit equivalent is the factor upon which our evaluation of the esthetic unity will usually depend. For example, it would not be esthetically satisfying if the death of the hero simply arrived without any particular climax preceding it. We need to feel the building of certain emotions which are responsible for the catastrophe, and without such a building we feel cheated.

4. Relations of Parts to Whole

In all of these approaches, and in countless others which the student will be able to devise for himself, we are concerned in one way or another with the relationship between the parts and the whole. We want to arrive at an understanding of structure by dividing a work, putting it back together, shaking it, and finally coming up with explanations of how it "works." We want to be able to say this play has the following structure and this is why it is or is not successful. Any given scene or act should contribute significantly to the overall structure of a play, for a play is too short for much waste of time. In other words, we address ourselves to the relationship between each of the parts and the whole in order to arrive at an understanding of the whole.

Some critics follow the general approach to the construction of Shakespeare's tragedies outlined and developed by A. C. Bradley in his famous lectures. Bradley explains how a Shakespearean tragedy always depicts some sort of *conflict* between competing forces which ends in *catastrophe*. Every play has three large parts. The first is the *exposition* or early part of the play where the dramatist presents us with certain information, introduces us to the world of the drama and to the characters. The second section is devoted to the complication or *conflict*— its beginnings, changes, reversals of advantage between the competing forces—and the third shows us the results of the conflict, that is, the catastrophe or conclusion. Often, Shakespeare gets the attention of his audience in the opening of a play with a dramatic event—such as the appearance of the ghost of Hamlet's father—and then slows the pace to provide us with certain necessary facts, usually presented through low-keyed conversations with little background action. In short, though, Shakespeare maintains the conflict throughout the play in various ways. There is constant alternation between our fears and our hopes as first one side is up, then another opposing one gathers momentum. The large three-fold way of viewing the construction of a Shakespearean play is often very useful, although not all of his plays fit the three-part division easily.

Questions and Answers on Structure

Question 5.

Outline the purpose and major events of each act, as they relate to the structure of *Hamlet*.

Answer

As in all of Shakespeare's plays, *Hamlet* is divided into five acts.

ACT I: INTRODUCTION: The setting (time and place) of the action is presented, and we are introduced to the central themes and characters of the play.

ACT II: DEVELOPMENT: Hamlet's plan to pretend that he is mad is put into action; Claudius schemes with Polonius to uncover the reasons behind Hamlet's strange behavior.

ACT III: CLIMAX: The Mouse-trap is "sprung" and Claudius is proven guilty (at least to Hamlet's satisfaction); Polonius is killed; the queen breaks down under Hamlet's merciless indictment.

ACT IV: DENOUNCEMENT: The results of the crisis and the procession of events toward the final catastrophe are presented. Hamlet is sent to England; Ophelia becomes insane and then dies; Laertes returns and becomes a party to Claudius' plot to kill Hamlet.

ACT V: CONCLUSION: The play moves swiftly towards a final catastrophe involving the deaths of all the chief characters, except Horatio and Fortinbras.

Question 6.

In what way can Fortinbras be considered a character whose chief function in the play is to serve its structural demands?

Answer

It is significant that the play is framed between the military preparations of Fortinbras, mentioned in the first scene, and the timely arrival of Fortinbras in the final scene, when he claims the throne of Denmark and has Hamlet nobly carried from the stage with "soldiers' music and rites of war."

Hamlet and Fortinbras never actually meet during the play. Fortinbras is just spoken of in Act I, Sc. 1; he leaves before Hamlet enters in Act IV, Sc. 4; and he arrives at the Danish court just after Hamlet's death in the last scene. Yet Hamlet does come across Fortinbras' army in Act IV, Sc. 4, and this incident serves to contrast—both for the audience and for Hamlet himself—the daring, honorable and assertive character of Fortinbras with the uncertain and aggressive Hamlet. Witnessing Fortinbras' troops preparing to fight for a cause which, to Hamlet, seems of so little concern, inspires the Danish prince to renew his efforts to seek revenge on Claudius for a cause which is of comparably greater importance. In Fortinbras' efforts to regain his father's lost territory and Hamlet's struggle to avenge the wrongs committed against his father by Claudius, there is an evident parallel. Each son accomplishes his mission by the end of the play, and though Hamlet forfeits his life for this purpose, he dies an honorable death, as Fortinbras confirms when he accords Hamlet soldiers' rites. It is by Fortinbras that we can measure the change in Hamlet from the adolescent scholar at the beginning of the play, to the young man more mature in thought and prepared for action in Act IV, Sc. 4, to the brave and heroic avenger figure he becomes just before his death.

Question 7.

The structure of drama is sometimes thought to be based on the principle of action followed by reaction. Cite examples in *Hamlet* of a character's own actions backfiring or reacting against him—a pattern that the Greeks called nemesis.

Answer

Hamlet's unsuspicious generosity is certainly mistaken in the last scene. He ought to have known his uncle by that time.

Gertrude's faithlessness to her husband's memory and her hasty marriage with this man she loves so madly, eventually brings about her death through his treachery to her son.

Claudius' original crime necessitates further crimes and he dies as a result of his own treachery by the hand of his nephew, the son of the man he murdered.

Polonius' passion for spying brings about his own death, quite unregretted by the audience, who are inclined to think, "served you right!"

Ophelia's too ready obedience to her petty-minded father starts the train of circumstances that lead to her insanity and death.

Laertes brings on his own death through his treacherous action in illegally removing the button from his foil and poisoning the point.

Notice that in each of the above instances, it is a character's own weakness that causes his undoing. This notion of a flaw in a person's character bringing disaster to that person is an important element in the working of nemesis.

Question 8.

What is the purpose of the graveyard scene in terms of the play's structure?

Answer

The graveyard scene is spectacular and gripping in itself, and though it does not advance the actual action of the play to any great extent, it provides a gleam of humor in this grim atmosphere. Further, it provides another lull before the last great storm. This scene also shows that Hamlet really was intensely in love with Ophelia and that he had purposely suppressed the romance while it interfered with his mission. He was a sufferer, too, though the effects of this whole situation were disastrous for her.

Question 9.

Classical tragedy observed what Aristotle called the *unity of time* (that is, the action of the tragedy was supposed to take place within one day). What length of time is covered in *Hamlet?*

Answer

The time of the play is seven days represented on the stage—or eight if the reader prefers to assign a separate day to the last scene—with two intervals.

Day 1: Act I, Scene 1 to Scene 3.
Day 2: Act I, Scene 4 and Scene 5.

An interval of over two months.

Day 3: Act II, Scene 1 and Scene 2.
Day 4: Act III, Scene 1 to Scene 4; Act IV, Scene 1 to Scene 3.
Day 5: Act IV, Scene 4.

An interval of perhaps a week.

Day 6: Act IV, Scene 5 to Scene 7.
Day 7: Act V, Scene 1 and Scene 2.

Meaning

Methods of Analyzing Meaning

Sometimes, it is noted, we forget about the forest because we are too busy looking at the individual trees. In this sense we are apt to avoid commenting on the fundamental meaning of a work of art because we are so concerned with character, structure, and style. Although it is obvious that we cannot avoid completely the implications of the various components of a play as they bear on its meaning, the fact remains that we should take the time to make some sort of general statement about what Shakespeare is trying to tell us. And once we have decided on the meaning, we then can attempt to evaluate the play, to measure it against other plays which treat the same ideas.

1. Explaining the Theme

The student's first task is to denote and explain the central theme of the play. This is not always easily done and, in fact, one sometimes must conclude that there are several themes combined throughout the play. Sometimes—but not often—there is no theme at all. The theme is the central and major idea of the work; in drama the theme is usually an abstract idea or argument which becomes real and concrete through the actions of the characters; as critics we must translate action back into thought, just as the playwright first translated thought into action.

2. Conventions
Usually the dramatist transports us into the world of the play through various dramatic conventions. We must ask how we, the audience, are transported into the minds of the characters. We must try to determine how we are made to believe certain ideas—how, in other words, does the dramatist convince us of the meaning of something? If we are led to believe that love is evil, how does the dramatist lead us to this belief? Meaning is not something easily determined and its presentation must often be clearly understood in order for us to determine precisely *why* such-and-such appears to be true.

3. Unusual or Conventional
The student must answer a basic question when discussing meaning: is it a conventional idea or an unusual one? For example, if the theme of the play is that revenge often only leads to further misery, we can speak of the theme as being "conventional." That is, the idea of the play is one which has been presented many times; it is an *established theme*. On the other hand, a play's main point might be very unusual. If a play's argument is that people who live in glass houses *should* throw stones, the play is making an unusual or uncommon point. Almost every play can be described, in its meaning, as being either conventional or unconventional; and once this is done, the student must explain the ways in which it is or is not conventional.

4. Relating Plot to Meaning
Probably the best way to begin one's analysis of the meaning of a play is to trace very briefly the main plot development in the play. In other words, we need to make a short synopsis of the action before we can make a general statement about the meaning. Then, as we become more particular in our comments on the meaning, we should introduce more particular use of the plot; in other words, we are concerned with making the *level* of our analysis correspond to the level of our explication of the plot. The broad statement needs a broad grasp of the plot, while the "fine points" need more particular textual backing.

5. Logic
As a final check on our understanding of the play we should make some attempt to ascertain whether or not the meaning is logically developed. If the theme somehow seems contradicted by the behavior of one or more characters, or if the relationship between two of the characters argues against the main idea of the play, then we have a problem of logic—which can mean either that the dramatist has not done an expert job, or that we have misunderstood the meaning of the play. If

our "interpretation" of a play is correct, we should be able to demonstrate logically why it is correct, while, on the other hand, if our interpretation is incorrect, a final check of the logic will force us into reconsideration and probably a revised, improved understanding of the play.

Questions and Answers on Meaning

Question 10.
Relate Hamlet's mental development to the meaning of the play.

Answer
To trace the steps by which Hamlet arrives at a resolution to his uncertain state of mind is, according to Hardin Craig, to master the meaning of the play. Hamlet progresses towards both action and the achievement of peace of mind, with Horatio standing on one side of him as a man who has self-possession, and Fortinbras on the other as a man to whom action is instinctive. It is through Hamlet's struggle to act, and to act wisely, that the larger concept of man's complex nature is illustrated.

The soliloquies in the play mark the stages of Hamlet's mental development. The first soliloquy in Act I, Scene 2, 129-59 shows Hamlet to be outraged at the treachery of Claudius and the "incestuous" marriage of his mother, but he is unable to act upon his convictions. After meeting with the Ghost, who prompts Hamlet to seek revenge, he is determined to act; however, Hamlet's feelings at this point (Act I, Scene 5, 97-112) are not guided by reason. Action alone will not satisfy the demands on Hamlet, since it is wise and appropriate action that he must undertake. In the famous "To be or not to be" soliloquy, Hamlet's excitement is calmed, and he achieves a balance between action and inaction when he wonders:

> Whether 'tis nobler in the mind to suffer
> The slings and arrows of outrageous fortune,
> Or to take arms against a sea of troubles,
> And by opposing end them?

Hamlet then progresses to the point of being overcalculating in Act III, Scene 3, 73-96, when he deliberately delays murdering Claudius at prayer because to kill the king now would "this same villain send /To heaven." Despite Hamlet's expressed concern with commiting the act properly, he acts rashly when he kills Polonius in Act III, Scene 4, and after this mistaken deed, a period of inaction on Hamlet's part follows. But after witnessing the marching of troops commanded by Fortinbras, Hamlet, in another soliloquy (Act IV, Scene 4, 32-66), once again recognizes the need to "spur [his] dull revenge." In Act V,

Hamlet's conversation with Horatio in the churchyard regarding the value of life shows that he has attained a more philosophical state of mind. Later in this act, his bitter outburst at the grave of Ophelia reveals the full development of his passionate nature as well. By the end of the play, Hamlet demonstrates both the self-knowledge and spirit of action necessary to carry out his revenge on Claudius in a fitting manner.

Question 11.

How does the question of appearance and reality affect the meaning of the play?

Answer

A major question for man is: What is truth? It involves such further questions as what is reality? How does one separate what appears to be truthful or real or absolute from what actually is? How can one determine what actually is truthful or real or absolute? During the Elizabethan Age the question was most compelling because of the advances of science. The certainties of the past were being disproved or at least modified. New celestial bodies were being discovered; new means of combating illnesses were being found; new concepts of the earth and its inhabitants came with the expansion of navigational exploration; and new views of God's creation necessarily followed. With universes beyond the no longer geocentric universe of medieval tradition, where could man place himself in the scheme of creation? The Englishman was only one man of many on earth; the earth was only one planet of many in the universe; the universe was only one in how many universes. That which was truth had been shown not to be truth.

In *Hamlet* the problems of truth and the nature of man appear on every page: Is the ghost good or evil? Is his story true or false? Is Hamlet's madness real or feigned? Is Polonius' advice wisdom or folly? Is his interpretation of Hamlet's relationship with Ophelia correct? Is she innocent or loose of character? The way in which appearance is taken for reality is underscored by the acting of Polonius, Rosencrantz, Guildenstern, and Hamlet, and by the play-within-a-play and the discussion of plays and actors. Should "this goodly frame, the earth," be thought a "most excellent canopy . . . fretted with golden fire" or "a sterile promontory . . . a foul and pestilent congregation of vapours" (Act II, Sc. 2, 306 ff.)? Hamlet follows these questions with musings on man: "what is this quintessence of dust?" He concludes (Act IV, Sc. 4) that a man is one who uses his capability and godlike reason; that person is a beast who simply sleeps and feeds. Hamlet has come to realize that man is noble in reason and the paragon of animals when he finds "quarrel in a straw/When honor's at the stake." Truth seems to reside in the existential idea: all that individual man knows is that he exists. For man truth can be only that which magnifies him in moral spheres. The essence of truth is thus divorced from substance and from the means through which substance appears.

Question 12.

Consider the theme of honor as it relates to the characters and actions of Hamlet, Laertes, and Fortinbras.

Answer

The parallel situations of Hamlet, Laertes, and Fortinbras examine the theme of honor and honorable action. Each seeks a restitution of loss from the death of a father, but the course that each takes is to be evaluated by the audience. Laertes seeks revenge known as *lex talionis*, "an eye for an eye;" but what casts this retributive justice into disrepute is the deceptive and murderous means by which he hopes to achieve justice: poison-tipped foils. This action can be classified only as evil: to seek to avenge a wrong by vicious action is abhorrent. Laertes does not "duplicate" Hamlet's ill action against Polonius (nor should he), thereby nullifying it, if successful. His honorable course would be challenge but without deceit. Fortinbras' course is an honorable one: he acts to regain the position of fame and material being that his father had. He accepts a challenge in the same sphere of action which his father had made and lost. His course is reasoned and public, but it does involve "the imminent death of twenty thousand men . . . for a fantasy and trick of fame" (Act IV, Sc. 4, 60-61).

Hamlet's course alters from indecision to action pulled in two directions. First, it is tempered by demands of proof; second, it is influenced by reason and then by emotion; third, it is necessary to reverse deception, and to make and accept challenge, first emotionally and then rationally. The need for proof places Hamlet in a different situation from those of Laertes and Fortinbras. His emotional course echoes Laertes', and his reversal of the king's deceptive act has similarities to Laertes' villainy. The results of the first are unjustified, and thus we see emotional response as wrong; but the results of the second are justified, and thus we see reasoned response as acceptable. Note that after acceptance of the king's guilt, Hamlet moves from reason (the prayer scene) to emotion (the killing of Polonius) to reasoned resolution, followed by acts of reason (the dispatch of Rosencrantz and Guildenstern), emotion (the argument at Ophelia's grave), and reason (the duel).

The theme of honor makes clear that action to correct a wrong should be reasoned, not emotional; it should be a reversal of the wrong as exactly as is honorably possible; and it should partake of public action and particularly that considered noble and commanding of respect. God's justice is accomplished by the various deaths and the ascendancy of Fortinbras to the throne. Hamlet can not live and have justice prevail, for he has erred in killing Polonius. Yet his death is ennobled by his final honorable actions in correcting the sources of rottenness within the state.

Question 13.
How is the theme of love presented in *Hamlet?*

Answer
For the most part faith is missing from *Hamlet*. The king, the queen, Rosencrantz, Guildenstern, Polonius, and Laertes are not trustworthy; the ghost's truthfulness must be established; and Ophelia proves unfaithful to Hamlet. Only Horatio is to be trusted and remains faithful. Without faith love cannot exist. Polonius talks a great deal about Ophelia and Hamlet's love, but all, including Ophelia, do not recognize his statements of faith and love in his letter read to the court by Polonius.

On the other hand there is Ophelia's obedience to her father and her remorse at his death; and there is the compassion of the player for Hecuba. In the final act we hear Hamlet coming to an answer for his question, "what is this quintessence of dust," as he observes the gravedigger and the noble dust of one who might have been an Alexander. The concept of love which is missing in Hamlet's makeup and which is developed in the play is charity, or brotherly love. Hamlet seeks Laertes' pardon and specifically cites his own abuse of charity: "I have shot my arrow o'er the house/And hurt my brother" (Act V, Sc. 2). His professed love of Ophelia has not exhibited charity, nor has his interview with his mother.

Style

Methods of Analyzing Style
When we address ourselves to the problems of style, we are, in effect, addressing ourselves to a relatively large group of components rather than to a single entity. Style is the basic verbal presentation of ideas and, in particular, the ways in which one specified author or dramatist *chooses* to express his ideas. Under the heading of style we place such components as arrangement, diction, rhythm, emphasis, figurative language, imagery, abstractions, etc. The best place to begin, it would seem, is with a consideration of diction.

1. Diction
Diction is the choice of words in expressing ideas. The words themselves constitute what we term a "vocabulary," while diction has to do with how the words of this vocabulary are chosen. In John Knowles' well-known novel, *A Separate Peace,* for example, the diction is military: that is, ideas are expressed in terms of war and the vocabulary of war is employed. In *Macbeth,* there is a great deal of the

vocabulary of witchcraft and many of the ideas are presented in terms suggestive of mystery and horror. Diction refers only to the selection of the words; the manner in which the author arranges them constitutes the essence of his particular style.

2. Imagery

In works of art we discover various "images" or representations of objects and people which somehow educate our senses. An image is a figure of speech employed in such a way that something comes to have a greater meaning than is implied in its literal sense. If throughout a play or a poem we find a linking between light and goodness, while at the same time we find an association of evil with darkness, we can then speak of the imagery of light and darkness. If many images of a similar nature are used we can begin to speak of various "patterns of imagery." For example, in Dickens' long novel *Bleak House,* every character is slowly associated with either an animal that is predatory or an animal which is meek and preyed upon. Thus we can speak of the imagery of hunting, or of imprisonment.

3. Figurative Language

An author places his own particular stamp on his work by employing figurative language. That is, the author communicates ideas to us by way of *analogies.* In a certain "figure" the poet presents one thing on the surface while very directly implying something else beneath the surface. The most common figures are the simile and the metaphor. In a simile, the poet or writer says that "X is *like* (or as) Y," while in a metaphor, the poet says "X is Y," in both cases hoping to increase our appreciation for something by showing us something analagous to it. "My love is a rose" is a metaphor which suggests to us the beauty and the developing freshness of love by associating love with a rose. Throughout most works of literature we discover figures of speech and although metaphors and similes are the most common, the student should also acquaint himself with other figures such as "antithesis," "personification," "metonymy," "synecdoche," and "hyperbole."

4. Emphasis

The principle behind "emphasis" is simply that the writer should devote the right amount of attention to what is more important; that is, the time spent on certain ideas should correspond roughly to the importance of those ideas within the work. The sequence of presentation is important, but the main consideration is that the author does not spend a disproportionate amount of time on something trivial or, conversely, insufficient time on what is of major importance. Furthermore, when we consider emphasis as a component of an author's style, we should try to notice how detail is subordinated to the larger ideas.

Put another way, we need to concentrate on the relationship of detail to what is universally implied. This leads us into a consideration of what is *general* and what is *particular*. We should single out some of the major statements of the theme, and then demonstrate their general truth by noting the ways in which particular statements support them.

5. Point of View

One aspect of style not discernible as easily in a play, but often of central importance to the understanding of a novel or a poem, is "point of view." We explain the attitude which the narrator or poet has toward his material. Further, what is the perspective of the poet? Is he writing about something in the past? If so, how far into the past? Is he sad about what happened? In short, by posing a series of questions we try to discover the writer's basic feelings behind the narration of the story; by explaining the position of the narrator we automatically describe the ways in which we can talk about a particular literary work.

6. Subjective Elements of Style

As style concerns the ways in which one particular author offers us a set of ideas, we must explain precisely what is particular about his methods. What are the private and personal feelings which shade all of the material? Is Shakespeare, for example, abnormally hateful of jealousy and is this hatred reflected in his style? Does the author have an anti-feminism which can be seen evidenced in certain stylistic excesses? This leads to a final consideration.

7. Comparing to Style of Other Works by Same Author

Because we are interested primarily in making conclusions about the style of one particular work and not about the author, we should try to discover what is unique about the style of one of his works. By comparing the style of the work with which we are concerned with the style of other works by the same author, we can either make generalizations about the author's style, or else explain what is stylistically unique about the particular work in question.

Questions and Answers on Style

Question 14.
Identify some of the chief characteristics of style in *Hamlet*.

Answer
When *Hamlet* (as we know it) was written, Shakespeare had left behind him those early years of authorship when his plays were rhyming poems and his imagery was mere decoration; he had passed through the period of transition (e.g. *Romeo and Juliet* and *Richard II*) which still showed many marks of immaturity. In *Hamlet* Shakespeare

shows himself to be a master craftsman. The early scenes of the play are remarkable for their rapid dialogue in verse, in which the supernatural is realistically brought into contact with the real. The prose, which is used liberally throughout the play, contains several masterful pieces of rhetoric. The soliloquies are excellent examples of slow, contemplative verse, and are very appropriate to the expression of thought in solitude. Like other plays by Shakespeare, *Hamlet* is also remarkable for its wealth of imagery, and especially for its use of metaphor. Note, for example, Act III, Sc. 3, 11-23, where three successive images express the same thought, and Act III, Sc. 4, 40-51, where the metaphors "are flaming apparitions, which are like a picture in a flash of lightning."

Question 15.

Discuss Hamlet's language in terms of his use of allusion and imagery.

Answer

In addition to thematic motifs that unify the play, *Hamlet* is integrated by specific allusions and image patterns. Hamlet's keen observation of the world around him is demonstrated in his many references to antiquity, courtier life, falconry, fine arts, military life, natural science and mythology. His intellectuality and intelligence, his social bearing and his interest in contemporary events reflect his character and help us recognize the tension he must experience in pursuing the course of action necessary to revenge. Hamlet's speech, beginning on line 54 of Act III, Sc. 4, reveals his extensive knowledge of mythology. He mentions *Hyperion's curls, the front of Jove himself, An eye like Mars* and *the herald Mercury* in the space of only three lines.

The recurrent image patterns in Hamlet's speech consist of references to disease and decay (representing corruption) and to human parts (emphasizing the animal, not angelic, side of man). In the same speech cited above, Hamlet refers to *a mildew'd ear, Blasting,* sense that is *apoplex'd, madness, a sickly part of one true sense,* and a few lines later, *rank sweat,* an *enseamed bed* and *Stewed in corruption.* Images relating to parts of the body are contained in references to *brow, curls, front, bones, eyes* (four times), and *ears.* Notice also the language of Claudius' prayer in Act III, Sc. 3, 36-71: *rank, smells, corrupted, wretched state, black as death, limed soul; hand, blood, teeth, forehead, bosom, knees, heart* and *sinews.* The pattern of disease and decay evoked in both Hamlet's and Claudius' speeches correlates with the rottenness of the state (of which these two characters are most consciously aware), the deceit and faithlessness underlying the action, and the multiple deaths. The pattern of human parts, on the other hand, points to the theme of man and his nature.

Question 16.
Account for the use of prose throughout so much of Act III, Scene 2, which deals largely with the arrival and performance of the players.

Answer
It has been commented earlier (See Shakespeare's Artistry) that the usual vehicle of Shakespeare's plays is iambic pentameter verse, unrhymed or 'blank.' Prose is used to denote a change in, usually a lowering of, dramatic pitch, a character speaking out of his natural part, outside matter (such as letters), and the speeches of characters of lower social rank.

In this act, most of the prose is of a higher character than that used elsewhere to provide comic relief. In the early part of the act, the use of prose shows the contrast between Hamlet when he is his natural self and Hamlet when he has assumed the appearance of madness. In conversation with Rosencrantz and Guildenstern, there is a contrast between Hamlet the fellow-student and Hamlet the prince. In conversation with the Players, there may be two reasons for the use of prose: to mark the degree of familiarity that exists between Hamlet and his old friend, and to strengthen the contrast between the dramatic play of *Hamlet* and the epic tragedy of Gonzago.

It should be noted, however, that some of the prose of this act, such as Hamlet's speech regarding "What a piece of work is a man," is very highly crafted and is more full of concentrated meaning than almost any of the blank verse of the play.

Question 17.
Cite examples from this drama of plays on words (puns).

Answer
Of the numerous examples of puns that are to be found in this play, the following are some of the most obvious:
1. On *kin* and *kind* (Act I, Sc. 2).
2. On three meanings of *tender* (Act I, Sc. 3).
3. On *Capitol* and *capital, Brutus* and *Brute* (Act III, Sc. 2).
4. On two meanings of *fret* (Act III, Sc. 2).
5. On the different meanings of *fine* (Act V, Sc. 1).
6. On two meanings of *assurance* (Act V, Sc. 1).
7. On two meanings of *lie* and *quick* (Act V, Sc. 1).
8. On two meanings of *ground* (Act V, Sc. 1).
9. On two meanings of *foil* (Act V, Sc. 2).

Question 18.
Discuss the poetic merits of Hamlet's soliloquy in Act II, Scene 2, which begins "O, what a rogue and peasant slave am I."

Answer

This soliloquy is in iambic pentameter blank (unrhymed) verse whose language is personal and direct, giving an effect of unrehearsed spontaneity. The poetic merits are many and varied, but two stand out: the effective imagery ("murder, though it hath no tongue, will speak/ With most miraculous organ") in which the crime, murder, is personi- fied, and alliteration of the m - sounds sustains the effect; and the dramatic intermingling of the *two* voices of Hamlet, that of the calm, reasonable aristocrat (as in "O, what a rogue and peasant slave am I!") contrasted with that of the passionate, disturbed man (as in "this slave's offal;"). Hamlet realizes that he has been speaking out of char- acter when he accuses himself of having had to

> unpack my heart with words,
> And fall a cursing, like a very drab.
> A scullion.

This intermixing by Shakespeare of courtly vocabulary and syntax with household cursing, in a single soliloquy, is a very effective poetic device, because it reveals Hamlet's mind working at at least two levels when trying to resolve his tragic conflict.

*The World of *Hamlet*

My subject is the world of *Hamlet*. I do not of course mean Den- mark, except as Denmark is given a body by the play; and I do not mean Elizabethan England, though this is necessarily close behind the scenes. I mean simply the imaginative environment that the play asks us to enter when we read it or go to see it.

Great plays, as we know, do present us with something that can be called a world, a microcosm—a world like our own in being made of people, actions, situations, thoughts, feelings, and much more, but unlike our own in being perfectly, or almost perfectly, significant and coherent. In a play's world, each part implies the other parts, and each lives, each means, with the life and meaning of the rest.

This is the reason, as we also know, that the worlds of great plays greatly differ. Othello in Hamlet's position, we sometimes say, would have no problem; but what we are really saying is that Othello in Ham- let's position would not exist. The conception we have of Othello is a function of the characters who help define him, Desdemona, honest Iago, Cassio, and the rest; of his history of travel and war; of a great storm that divides his ship from Cassio's, and a handkerchief; of a quiet night in Venice broken by cries about an old black ram; of a quiet night in Cyprus broken by swordplay; of a quiet bedroom where a

*By Maynard Mack. From *The Yale Review,* XLI (1952).

woman goes to bed in her wedding sheets and a man comes in with a light to put out the light; and above all, of a language, a language with many voices in it, gentle, rasping, querulous, or foul, but all counterpointing the one great voice:

> Put up your bright swords, for the dew will rust them.[1]

>> O thou weed
> Who art so lovely fair and smell'st so sweet
> That the sense aches at thee. . . .[2]

>> Yet I'll not shed her blood
> Nor scar that whiter skin of hers than snow,
> And smooth as monumental alabaster.[3]

>> I pray you in your letters,
> When you shall these unlucky deeds relate,
> Speak of me as I am; nothing extenuate,
> Nor set down aught in malice; then must you speak
> Of one that loved not wisely but too well;
> Of one not easily jealous, but being wrought,
> Perplex'd in th' extreme; of one whose hand,
> Like the base Indian, threw a pearl away
> Richer than all his tribe. . . .[4]

Without his particular world of voices, persons, events, the world that both expresses and contains him, Othello is unimaginable. And so, I think, are Antony, King Lear, Macbeth—and Hamlet. We come back then to Hamlet's world, of all the tragic worlds that Shakespeare made, easily the most various and brilliant, the most elusive. It is with no thought of doing justice to it that I have singled out three of its attributes for comment. I know too well, if I may echo a sentiment of Mr. E. M. W. Tillyard's, that no one is likely to accept another man's reading of *Hamlet,* that anyone who tries to throw light on one part of the play usually throws the rest into deeper shadow, and that what I have to say leaves out many problems—to mention only one, the knotty problem of the text. All I would say in defense of the materials I have chosen is that they seem to be interesting, close to the root of the matter even if we continue to differ about what the root of the matter is, and explanatory, in a modest way, of this play's peculiar hold on everyone's imagination, its almost mythic status, one might say, as a paradigm of the life of man.

The first attribute that impresses us, I think, is mysteriousness. We often hear it said, perhaps with truth, that every great work of art has a mystery at the heart; but the mystery of *Hamlet* is something else. We feel its presence in the numberless explanations that have been

122

brought forward for Hamlet's delay, his madness, his ghost, his treatment of Polonius, or Ophelia, or his mother; and in the controversies that still go on about whether the play is "undoubtedly a failure" (Eliot's phrase) or one of the greatest artistic triumphs; whether, if it is a triumph, it belongs to the highest order of tragedy; whether, if it is such a tragedy, its hero is to be taken as a man of exquisite moral sensibility (Bradley's view) or an egomaniac (Madariaga's view).

Doubtless there have been more of these controversies and explanations than the play requires; for in Hamlet, to paraphrase a remark of Falstaff's, we have a character who is not only mad in himself but a cause that madness is in the rest of us. Still, the very existence of so many theories and counter-theories, many of them formulated by sober heads, gives food for thought. *Hamlet* seems to lie closer to the illogical logic of life than Shakespeare's other tragedies. And while the causes of this situation may be sought by saying that Shakespeare revised the play so often that eventually the motivations were smudged over, or that the original old play has been here or there imperfectly digested, or that the problems of Hamlet lay so close to Shakespeare's heart that he could not quite distance them in the formal terms of art, we have still as critics to deal with effects, not causes. If I may quote again from Mr. Tillyard, the play's very lack of a rigorous type of causal logic seems to be a part of its point.

Moreover, the matter goes deeper than this. Hamlet's world is pre-eminently in the interrogative mood. It reverberates with questions, anguished, meditative, alarmed. There are questions that in this play, to an extent I think unparalleled in any other, mark the phases and even the nuances of the action, helping to establish its peculiar baffled tone. There are other questions whose interrogations, innocent at first glance, are subsequently seen to have reached beyond their contexts and to point towards some pervasive inscrutability in Hamlet's world as a whole. Such is that tense series of challenges with which the tragedy begins: Bernardo's of Francisco, "Who's there?" Francisco's of Horatio and Marcellus, "Who is there?" Horatio's of the ghost, "What art thou . . . ?" And then there are the famous questions. In them the interrogations seem to point not only beyond the context but beyond the play, out of Hamlet's predicaments into everyone's: "What a piece of work is a man! . . . And yet to me what is this quintessence of dust?" "To be, or not to be, that is the question." "Get thee to a nunnery. Why wouldst thou be a breeder of sinners?" "I am very proud, revengeful, ambitious, with more offences at my beck than I have thoughts to put them in, imagination to give them shape, or time to act them in. What should such fellows as I do crawling between earth and heaven?" "Dost thou think Alexander look'd o' this fashion i' th' earth? . . . And smelt so?"

Further, Hamlet's world is a world of riddles. The hero's own language is often riddling, as the critics have pointed out. When he puns, his puns have receding depths in them, like the one which constitutes his first speech: "A little more than kin, and less than kind." His utterances in madness, even if wild and whirling, are simultaneously, as Polonius discovers, pregnant: "Do you know me, my lord?" "Excellent well. You are a fishmonger." Even the madness itself is riddling: How much is real? How much is feigned? What does it mean? Sane or mad, Hamlet's mind plays restlessly about his world, turning up one riddle upon another. The riddle of character, for example, and how it is that in a man whose virtues else are "pure as grace," some vicious mole of nature, some "dram of eale," can "all the noble substance oft adulter." Or the riddle of the player's art, and how a man can so project himself into a fiction, a dream of passion, that he can weep for Hecuba. Or the riddle of action: how we may think too little—"What to ourselves in passion we propose," says the player-king, "The passion ending, doth the purpose lose;" and again, how we may think too much: "Thus conscience does make cowards of us all, And thus the native hue of resolution Is sicklied o'er with the pale cast of thought."

There are also more immediate riddles. His mother—how could she "on this fair mountain leave to feed, And batten on this moor?" The ghost—which may be a devil, for "the de'il hath power T' assume a pleasing shape." Ophelia—what does her behavior to him mean? Surprising her in her closet, he falls to such perusal of her face as he would draw it. Even the king at his prayers is a riddle. Will a revenge that takes him in the purging of his soul be vengeance, or hire and salary? As for himself, Hamlet realizes, he is the greatest riddle of all—a mystery, he warns Rosencrantz and Guildenstern, from which he will not have the heart plucked out. He cannot tell why he has of late lost all his mirth, forgone all custom of exercises. Still less can he tell why he delays: "I do not know Why yet I live to say, 'This thing's to do,' Sith I have cause and will and strength and means To do 't."

Thus the mysteriousness of Hamlet's world is of a piece. It is not simply a matter of missing motivations, to be expunged if only we could find the perfect clue. It is built in. It is evidently an important part of what the play wishes to say to us. And it is certainly an element that the play thrusts upon us from the opening word. Everyone, I think, recalls the mysteriousness of that first scene. The cold middle of the night on the castle platform, the muffled sentries, the uneasy atmosphere of apprehension, the challenges leaping out of the dark, the questions that follow the challenges, feeling out the darkness, searching for identities, for relations, for assurance. "Bernardo?" "Have you had quiet guard?" "Who hath reliev'd you?" "What, is Horatio there?" "What, has this thing appear'd again tonight?" "Looks 'a not like the king?" "How now, Horatio! . . . Is not this something more than fantasy? What think you on 't?" "It is not like the king?" "Why this same strict and most observant watch . . . ?" "Shall I strike at it with my partisan?'' "Do you consent we shall acquaint [young Hamlet] with it?''

We need not be surprised that critics and playgoers alike have been tempted to see in this an evocation not simply of Hamlet's world but of their own. Man in his aspect of bafflement, moving in darkness on a rampart between two worlds, unable to reject, or quite accept, the one that, when he faces it, "to-shakes" his disposition with thoughts beyond the reaches of his soul—comforting himself with hints and guesses. We hear these hints and guesses whispering through the darkness as the several watchers speak. "At least, the whisper goes so,'' says one. "I think it be no other but e'en so,'' says another. "I have heard" that on the crowing of the cock "Th' extravagant and erring spirit hies To his confine,'' says a third. "Some say" at Christmas time "this bird of dawning" sings all night, "And then, they say, no spirit dare stir abroad.'' "So have I heard,'' says the first, "and do in part believe it.'' However we choose to take the scene, it is clear that it creates a world where uncertainties are of the essence.

Meantime, such is Shakespeare's economy, a second attribute of Hamlet's world has been put before us. This is the problematic nature of reality and the relation of reality to appearance. The play begins with an appearance, an "apparition,'' to use Marcellus's term—the ghost. And the ghost is somehow real, indeed the vehicle of realities. Through its revelation, the glittering surface of Claudius's court is pierced, and Hamlet comes to know, and we do, that the king is not only hateful to him but the murderer of his father, that his mother is guilty of adultery as well as incest. Yet there is a dilemma in the revelation. For possibly the apparition *is* an apparition, a devil who has assumed his father's shape.

This dilemma, once established, recurs on every hand. From the court's point of view, there is Hamlet's madness. Polonius investigates and gets some strange advice about his daughter: "Conception is a blessing, but as your daughter may conceive, friend, look to 't.'' Rosencrantz and Guildenstern investigate and get the strange confidence that "Man delights not me; no, nor woman neither.'' Ophelia is "loosed" to Hamlet (Polonius's vulgar word), while Polonius and the king hide behind the arras; and what they hear is a strange indictment of human nature, and a riddling threat: "Those that are married already, all but one, shall live.''

On the other hand, from Hamlet's point of view, there is Ophelia. Kneeling here at her prayers, she seems the image of innocence and devotion. Yet she is of the sex for whom he has already found the name Frailty, and she is also, as he seems either madly or sanely to divine, a decoy in a trick. The famous cry—"Get thee to a nunnery"—shows the anguish of his uncertainty. If Ophelia is what she seems, this dirty-minded world of murder, incest, lust, adultery, is no place for her. Were she "as chaste as ice, as pure as snow,'' she could not escape its calumny. And if she is not what she seems, then a nunnery in its other sense of brothel is relevant to her. In the scene that follows he treats her as if she were indeed an inmate of a brothel.

Likewise, from Hamlet's point of view, there is the enigma of the king. If the ghost is *only* an appearance, then possibly the king's appearance is reality. He must try it further. By means of a second and different kind of "apparition," the play within the play, he does so. But then, immediately after, he stumbles on the king at prayer. This appearance has a relish of salvation in it. If the king dies now, his soul may yet be saved. Yet actually, as we know, the king's efforts to come to terms with heaven have been unavailing; his words fly up, his thoughts remain below. If Hamlet means the conventional revenger's reasons that he gives for sparing Claudius, it was the perfect moment not to spare him—when the sinner was acknowledging his guilt, yet unrepentant. The perfect moment, but it was hidden, like so much else in the play, behind an arras.

There are two arrases in his mother's room. Hamlet thrusts his sword through one of them. Now at last he has got to the heart of the evil, or so he thinks. But now it is the wrong man; now he himself is a murderer. The other arras he stabs through with his words—like daggers, says the queen. He makes her shrink under the contrast he points between her present husband and his father. But as the play now stands (matters are somewhat clearer in the bad Quarto), it is hard to be sure how far the queen grasps the fact that her second husband is the murderer of her first. And it is hard to say what may be signified by her inability to see the ghost, who now for the last time appears. In one sense at least, the ghost is the supreme reality, representative of the hidden ultimate power, in Bradley's terms—witnessing from beyond the grave against this hollow world. Yet the man who is capable of seeing through to this reality, the queen thinks is mad. "To whom do you speak this?" she cries to her son. "Do you see nothing there?" he asks, incredulous. And she replies: "Nothing at all; yet all that is I see." Here certainly we have the imperturbable self-confidence of the worldly world, its layers on layers of habituation, so that when the reality is before its very eyes it cannot detect its presence.

Like mystery, this problem of reality is central to the play and written deep into its idiom. Shakespeare's favorite terms in *Hamlet* are words of ordinary usage that pose the question of appearances in a fundamental form. "Apparition" I have already mentioned. Another term is "seems." When we say, as Ophelia says of Hamlet leaving her closet. "He seem'd to find his way without his eyes," we mean one thing. When we say, as Hamlet says to his mother in the first court-scene, "Seems, Madam! . . . I know not 'seems,'" we mean another. And when we say, as Hamlet says to Horatio before the play within the play, "And after, we will both our judgments join In censure of his seeming," we mean both at once. The ambiguities of "seem" coil and uncoil throughout this play, and over against them is set the idea of "seeing." So Hamlet challenges the king in his triumphant letter announcing his return to Denmark: "Tomorrow shall I beg leave to see your kingly eyes." Yet "seeing" itself can be ambiguous, as we recognize from Hamlet's uncertainty about the ghost; or from that statement of his mother's already quoted: "Nothing at all; yet all that is I see."

Another term of like importance is "assume." What we assume may be what we are not: "The de'il hath power T' assume a pleasing shape." But it may be what we are: "If it assume my noble father's person, I'll speak to it." And it may be what we are not yet, but would become; thus Hamlet advises his mother, "Assume a virtue, if you have it not." The perplexity in the word points to a real perplexity in Hamlet's and our own experience. We assume our habits—and habits are like costumes, as the word implies: "My father in his habit as he liv'd!" Yet these habits become ourselves in time: "That monster, custom, who all sense doth eat Of habits evil, is angel yet in this, That to the use of actions fair and good He likewise gives a frock or livery That aply is put on."

Two other terms I wish to instance are "put on" and "shape." The shape of something is the form under which we are accustomed to apprehend it: "Do you see yonder cloud that's almost in shape of a camel?" But a shape may also be a disguise—even, in Shakespeare's time, an actor's costume or an actor's role. This is the meaning when the king says to Laertes as they lay the plot against Hamlet's life: "Weigh that convenience both of time and means May fit us to our shape." "Put on" supplies an analogous ambiguity. Shakespeare's mind seems to worry this phrase in the play much as Hamlet's mind worries the problem of acting in a world of surfaces, or the king's mind worries the meaning of Hamlet's transformation. Hamlet has put an antic disposition on, that the king knows. But what does "put on" mean? A mask, or a frock or livery—our "habit"? The king is left guessing, and so are we.

What is found in the play's key terms is also found in its imagery. Miss Spurgeon has called attention to a pattern of disease images in *Hamlet,* to which I shall return. But the play has other patterns equally striking. One of these, as my earlier quotations hint, is based on clothes. In the world of surfaces to which Shakespeare exposes us in Hamlet, clothes are naturally a factor of importance. "The apparel oft proclaims the man," Polonius assures Laertes, cataloguing maxims in the young man's ear as he is about to leave for Paris. Oft, but not always. And so he sends his man Reynaldo to look into Laertes' life there—even, if need be, to put a false dress of accusation upon his son ("What forgeries you please"), the better by indirections to find directions out. On the same grounds, he takes Hamlet's vows to Ophelia a false apparel. They are bawds, he tells her—or if we do not like Theobald's emendation, they are bonds—in masquerade, "Not of that dye which their investments show, But mere implorators of unholy suits."

This breach between the outer and the inner stirs no special emotion in Polonius, because he is always either behind an arras or prying into one, but it shakes Hamlet to the core. Here so recently was his mother in her widow's weeds, the tears still flushing in her galled eyes; yet now within a month, a little month, before even her funeral shoes are old, she has married with his uncle. Her mourning was all clothes. Not so his own, he bitterly replies, when she asks him to cast his "nighted color off." "'Tis not alone my inky cloak, good mother"—and not alone, he adds, the sighs, the tears, the dejected havior of the visage—"that can denote me truly."

> These indeed seem,
> For they are actions that a man might play;
> But I have that within which passes show;
> These but the trappings and the suits of woe. [5]

What we must not overlook here is Hamlet's visible attire, giving the verbal imagery a theatrical extension. Hamlet's apparel now is his inky cloak, mark of his grief for his father, mark also of his character as a man of melancholy, mark possibly too of his being one in whom appearance and reality are attuned. Later, in his madness, with his mind disordered, he will wear his costume in a corresponding disarray, the disarray that Ophelia describes so vividly to Polonius and that producers of the play rarely give sufficient heed to: "Lord Hamlet with his doublet all unbrac'd, No hat upon his head; his stockings foul'd, Ungarter'd, and down-gyved to his ankle." Here the only question will be, as with the madness itself, how much is studied, how much is real. Still later, by a third costume, the simple traveler's garb in which we find him new come from shipboard. Shakespeare will show us that we have a third aspect of the man.

A second pattern of imagery springs from terms of painting: the paints, the colorings, the varnishes that may either conceal or, as in the painter's art, reveal. Art in Claudius conceals. "The harlot's cheek," he tells us in his one aside, "beautied with plastering art, Is not more ugly to the thing that helps it Than is my deed to my most painted word." Art in Ophelia, loosed to Hamlet in the episode already noticed to which this speech of the king's is prelude, is more complex. She looks so beautiful—"the celestial, and my soul's idol, the most beautified Ophelia," Hamlet has called her in his love letter. But now, what does beautified mean? Perfected with all the innocent beauties of a lovely woman? Or "beautied" like the harlot's cheek? "I have heard of your paintings too, well enough. God hath given you one face, and you make yourselves another."

Yet art, differently used, may serve the truth. By using an

"image" (his own word) of a murder done in Vienna, Hamlet cuts through to the king's guilt; holds "as 'twere, the mirror up to nature," shows "virtue her own feature, scorn her own image, and the very age and body of the time"—which is out of joint—"his form and pressure." Something similar he does again in his mother's bedroom, painting for her in words "the rank sweat of an enseamed bed," making her recoil in horror from his "counterfeit presentment of two brothers," and holding, if we may trust a stage tradition, his father's picture beside his uncle's. Here again the verbal imagery is realized visually on the stage.

The most pervasive of Shakespeare's image patterns in this play, however, is the pattern evolved around the three words, show, act, play. "Show" seems to be Shakespeare's unifying image in *Hamlet*. Through it he pulls together and exhibits in a single focus much of the diverse material in his play. The ideas of seeming, assuming, and putting on; the images of clothing, painting, mirroring; the episode of the dumb show and the play within the play; the characters of Polonius, Laertes, Ophelia, Claudius, Gertrude, Rosencrantz and Guildenstern, Hamlet himself—all these at one time or another, and usually more than once, are drawn into the range of implications flung round the play by "show."

"Act," on the other hand, I take to be the play's radical metaphor. It distills the various perplexities about the character of reality into a residual perplexity about the character of an act. What, this play asks again and again, is an act? What is its relation to the inner act, the intent? "If I drown myself wittingly," says the clown in the graveyard, "it argues an act, and an act hath three branches; it is to act, to do, to perform." Or again, the play asks, how does action relate to passion, that "laps'd in time and passion" I can let "go by Th' important acting of your dread command"; and to thought, which can so sickly o'er the native hue of resolution that "enterprises of great pitch and moment With this regard their currents turn awry, And lose the name of action"; and to words, which are not acts, and so we dare not be content to unpack our hearts with them, and yet are acts of a sort, for we may speak daggers though we use none. Or still again, how does an act (a deed) relate to an act (a pretense)? For an action may be nothing but pretense. So Polonius readying Ophelia for the interview with Hamlet, with "pious action," as he phrases it, "sugar[s] o'er The devil himself." Or it may not be a pretense, yet not what it appears. So Hamlet spares the king, finding him in an act that has some "relish of salvation in 't." Or it may be a pretense that is also the first foothold of a new reality, as when we assume a virtue though we have it not. Or it may be a pretense that is actually a mirroring of reality, like the play within the play, or the tragedy of *Hamlet*.

To this network of implications, the third term, play, adds an additional dimension. "Play" is a more precise word, in Elizabethan parlance at least, for all the elements in *Hamlet* that pertain to the art of the theatre; and it extends their field of reference till we see that every major personage in the tragedy is a player in some sense, and every major episode a play. The court plays, Hamlet plays, the players play, Rosencrantz and Guildenstern try to play on Hamlet, though they cannot play on his recorders—here we have an extension to a musical sense. And the final duel, by a further extension, becomes itself a play, in which everyone but Claudius and Laertes plays his role in ignorance: "The queen desires you to show some gentle entertainment to Laertes before you fall to play." "I . . . will this brother's wager frankly play." "Give him the cup."—"I'll play this bout first."

The full extension of this theme is best evidenced in the play within the play itself. Here, in the bodily presence of these traveling players, bringing with them the latest playhouse gossip out of London, we have suddenly a situation that tends to dissolve the normal barriers between the fictive and the real. For here on the stage before us is a play of false appearances in which an actor called the player-king is playing. But there is also on the stage, Claudius, another player-king, who is a spectator of this player. And there is on the stage, besides, a prince who is a spectator of both these player-kings and who plays with great intensity a player's role himself. And around these kings and that prince is a group of courtly spectators—Gertrude, Rosencrantz, Guildenstern, Polonius, and the rest—and they, as we have come to know, are players too. And lastly there are ourselves, an audience watching all these audiences who are also players. Where, it may suddenly occur to us to ask, does the playing end? Which *are* the guilty creatures sitting at a play? When is an act not an "act"?

The mysteriousness of Hamlet's world, while it pervades the tragedy, finds its point of greatest dramatic concentration in the first act, and its symbol in the first scene. The problems of appearance and reality also pervade the play as a whole, but come to a climax in Acts II and III, and possibly their best symbol is the play within the play. Our third attribute, though again it is one that crops out everywhere, reaches its full development in Acts IV and V. It is not easy to find an appropriate name for this attribute, but perhaps "mortality" will serve, if we remember to mean by mortality the heartache and the thousand natural shocks that flesh is heir to, not simply death.

The powerful sense of mortality in *Hamlet* is conveyed to us, I think, in three ways. First, there is the play's emphasis on human weakness, the instability of human purpose, the subjection of humanity to fortune—all that we might call the aspect of failure in man. Hamlet opens this theme in Act I, when he describes how from that single blemish, perhaps not even the victim's fault, a man's whole character may take corruption. Claudius dwells on it again, to an extent that goes far beyond the needs of the occasion, while engaged in seducing Laertes to step behind the arras of a seemer's world and dispose of Hamlet by a trick. Time qualifies everything, Claudius says, including love, including purpose. As for love—it has a "plurisy" in it and dies of its own too much. As for purpose—"That we would do, We should do when we would, for this 'would' changes, And hath abatements and delays as many As there are tongues, are hands, are accidents; And then this 'should' is like a spendthrift's sigh, That hurts by easing." The player-king, in his long speeches to his queen in the play within the play, sets the matter in a still darker light. She means these protestations of undying love, he knows, but our purposes depend on our memory, and our memory fades fast. Or else, he suggests, we propose something to ourselves in a condition of strong feeling, but then the feeling goes, and with it the resolve. Or else our fortunes change, he adds, and with these our loves: "The great man down, you mark his favorite flies." The subjection of human aims to fortune is a reiterated theme in *Hamlet*, as subsequently in *Lear*. Fortune is the harlot goddess in whose secret parts men like Rosencrantz and Guildenstern live and thrive; the strumpet who threw down Troy and Hecuba and Priam; the outrageous foe whose slings and arrows a man of principle must suffer or seek release in suicide. Horatio suffers them with composure: he is one of the blessed few "Whose blood and judgment are so well co-mingled That they are not a pipe for fortune's finger To sound what stop she please." For Hamlet the task is of a greater difficulty.

Next, and intimately related to this matter of infirmity, is the emphasis on infection—the ulcer, the hidden abscess, "th' imposthume of much wealth and peace That inward breaks and shows no cause without Why the man dies." Miss Spurgeon, who was the first to call attention to this aspect of the play, has well remarked that so far as Shakespeare's pictorial imagination is concerned, the problem in *Hamlet* is not a problem of the will and reason, "of a mind too philosophical or a nature temperamentally unfitted to act quickly," nor even a problem of an individual at all. Rather, it is a condition—"a condition for which the individual himself is apparently not responsible, any more than the sick man is to blame for the infection which strikes and devours him, but which, nevertheless, in its course and development, impartially and relentlessly, annihilates him and others, innocent and guilty alike." "That," she adds, "is the tragedy of *Hamlet*, as it is perhaps the chief tragic mystery of life." This is a perceptive comment, for it reminds us that Hamlet's situation is mainly not of his own manufacture, as are the situations of Shakespeare's other tragic heroes. He has inherited it; he is "born to set it right."

We must not, however, neglect to add to this what another student of Shakespeare's imagery has noticed—that the infection in Denmark is presented alternatively as poison. Here, of course, responsibility is implied, for the poisoner of the play is Claudius. The juice he pours into the ear of the elder Hamlet is a combined poison and disease, a "leperous distilment" that curds "the thin and wholesome blood." From this fatal center, unwholesomeness spreads out till there is something rotten in all Denmark. Hamlet tells us that his "wit's diseased," the queen speaks of her "sick soul," the king is troubled by "the hectic" in his blood, Laertes meditates revenge to warm "the sickness in my heart," the people of the kingdom grow "muddied, Thick and unwholesome in their thoughts"; and even Ophelia's madness is said to be "the poison of deep grief." In the end, all save Ophelia die of that poison in a literal as well as figurative sense.

But the chief form in which the theme of mortality reaches us, it seems to me, is as a profound consciousness of loss. Hamlet's father expresses something of the kind when he tells Hamlet how his "most seeming-virtuous queen," betraying a love which "was of that dignity That it went hand in hand even with the vow I made to her in marriage," had chosen to "decline Upon a wretch whose natural gifts were poor To those of mine." "O Hamlet, what a falling off was there!" Ophelia expresses it again, on hearing Hamlet's denunciation of love and woman in the nunnery scene, which she takes to be the product of a disordered brain:

> O what a noble mind is here o'erthrown!
> The courtier's, soldier's, scholar's, eye, tongue, sword;
> Th' expectancy and rose of the fair state,
> The glass of fashion and the mould of form,
> Th' observ'd of all observers, quite, quite down![6]

The passage invites us to remember that we have never actually seen such a Hamlet—that his mother's marriage has brought a falling off in him before we meet him. And then there is that further falling off, if I may call it so, when Ophelia too goes mad—"Divided from herself and her fair judgment, Without the which we are pictures, or mere beasts."

Time was, the play keeps reminding us, when Denmark was a different place. That was before Hamlet's mother took off "the rose From the fair forehead of an innocent love" and set a blister there. Hamlet then was still "th' expectancy and rose of the fair state"; Ophelia, the "rose of May." For Denmark was a garden then, when his father ruled. There had been something heroic about his father—a king who met the threats to Denmark in open battle, fought with Norway, smote the sledded Polacks on the ice, slew the elder Fortinbras in an honorable trial of strength. There had been something godlike about his father too: "Hyperion's curls, the front of Jove himself, An eye like Mars . . . , A station like the herald Mercury." But, the ghost reveals, a serpent was in the garden, and "the serpent that did sting thy father's life Now wears his crown." The martial virtues are put by now. The threats to Denmark are attended to by policy, by agents working deviously for and through an uncle. The moral virtues are put by too. Hyperion's throne is occupied by "a vice of kings," "a king of shreds and patches"; Hyperion's bed, by a satyr, a paddock, a bat, a gib, a bloat king with reechy kisses. The garden is unweeded now, and "grows to seed; things rank and gross in nature Possess it merely." Even in himself he feels the taint, the taint of being his mother's son; and that other taint, from an earlier garden, of which he admonishes Ophelia: "Our virtue cannot so inoculate our old stock but we shall relish of it." "Why wouldst thou be a breeder of sinners?" "What should such fellows as I do crawling between earth and heaven?"

"Hamlet is painfully aware," says Professor Tillyard, "of the baffling human predicament between the angels and the beasts, between the glory of having been made in God's image and the incrimination of being descended from fallen Adam." To this we may add, I think, that Hamlet is more than aware of it; he exemplifies it; and it is for this reason that his problem appeals to us so powerfully as an image of our own.

Hamlet's problem, in its crudest form, is simply the problem of the avenger; he must carry out the injunction of the ghost and kill the king. But this problem, as I ventured to suggest at the outset, is presented in terms of a certain kind of world. The ghost's injunction to act becomes so inextricably bound up for Hamlet with the character of the world in which the action must be taken—its mysteriousness, its baffling appearances, its deep consciousness of infection, frailty, and loss —that he cannot come to terms with either without coming to terms with both.

When we first see him in the play, he is clearly a very young man, sensitive and idealistic, suffering the first shock of growing up. He has taken the garden at face value, we might say, supposing mankind to be only a little lower than the angels. Now in his mother's hasty and incestuous marriage, he discovers evidence of something else, something bestial—though even a beast, he thinks, would have mourned longer. Then comes the revelation of the ghost, bringing a second shock. Not so much because he now knows that his serpent-uncle killed his father; his prophetic soul had almost suspected this. Not entirely, even, because he knows now how far below the angels humanity has fallen in his mother, and how lust—these were the ghost's words—"though to a radiant angel link'd Will sate itself in a celestial bed, And prey on garbage." Rather, because he now sees everywhere, but especially in his own nature, the general taint, taking from life its meaning, from woman her integrity, from the will its strength, turning reason into madness. "Why wouldst thou be a breeder of sinners?" "What should such fellows as I do crawling between earth and heaven?" Hamlet is not the first young man to have felt the heavy and the weary weight of

133

all this unintelligible word; and, like the others, he must come to terms with it.

The ghost's injunction to revenge unfolds a different facet of his problem. The young man growing up is not to be allowed simply to endure a rotten world, he must also act in it. Yet how to begin, among so many enigmatic surfaces? Even Claudius, whom he now knows to be the core of the ulcer, has a plausible exterior. And around Claudius, swathing the evil out of sight, he encounters all those other exteriors, as we have seen. Some of them already deeply infected beneath, like his mother. Some noble, but marked for infection, like Laertes. Some not particularly corrupt but infinitely corruptible, like Rosencrantz and Guildenstern; some mostly weak and foolish like Polonius and Osric. Some, like Ophelia, innocent, yet in their innocence still serving to "skin and film the ulcerous place."

And this is not all. The act required of him, through retributive justice, is one that necessarily involves the doer in the general guilt. Not only because it involves a killing; but because to get at the world of seeming one sometimes has to use its weapons. He himself, before he finishes, has become a player, has put an antic disposition on, has killed a man—the wrong man—has helped drive Ophelia mad, and has sent two friends of his youth to death, mining below their mines, and hoisting the engineer with his own petard. He had never meant to dirty himself with these things, but from the moment of the ghost's challenge to act, this dirtying was inevitable. It is the condition of living at all in such a world. To quote Polonius, who knew that world so well, men become "a little soil'd i' th' working." Here is another matter with which Hamlet has to come to terms.

Human infirmity—all that I have discussed with reference to instability, infection, loss—supplies the problem with its third phase. Hamlet has not only to accept the mystery of man's condition between the angels and the brutes, and not only to act in a perplexing and soiling world. He has also to act within the human limits—"with shabby equipment always deteriorating," if I may adapt some phrases from Eliot's "East Coker," "In the general mess of imprecision of feeling, Undisciplined squads of emotion." Hamlet is aware of that fine poise of body and mind, feeling and thought, that suits the action to the word, the word to the action; that acquires and begets a temperance in the very torrent, tempest, and whirlwind of passion; but he cannot at first achieve it in himself. He vacillates between undisciplined squads of emotion and thinking too precisely on the event. He learns to his cost how easily action can be lost in "acting," and loses it there for a time himself. But these again are only the terms of every man's life. As Anatole France reminds us in a now famous apostrophe to Hamlet: "What one of us thinks without contradiction and acts without incoherence? What one of us is not mad? What one of us does not say with a mixture of pity, comradeship, admiration, and horror, Goodnight, sweet Prince!''

In the last act of the play (or so it seems to me, for I know there can be differences on this point), Hamlet accepts his world and we discover a different man. Shakespeare does not outline for us the process of acceptance any more than he had done with Romeo or was to do with Othello. But he leads us strongly to expect an altered Hamlet, and then, in my opinion, provides him. We must recall that at this point Hamlet has been absent from the stage during several scenes, and that such absences in Shakespearean tragedy usually warn us to be on the watch for a new phase in the development of the character. It is so when we leave King Lear in Gloucester's farmhouse and find him again in Dover fields. It is so when we leave Macbeth at the witches' cave and rejoin him at Dunsinane, hearing of the armies that beset it. Furthermore, and this is an important matter in the theatre—especially important in a play in which the symbolism of clothing has figured largely—Hamlet now looks different. He is wearing a different dress—probably, as Granville-Barker, thinks, his "sea-gown scarf'd" about him, but in any case no longer the disordered costume of his antic disposition. The effect is not entirely dissimilar to that in *Lear,* when the old king wakes out of his madness to find fresh garments on him.

Still more important, Hamlet displays a considerable change of mood. This is not a matter of the way we take the passage about defying augury, as Mr. Tillyard among others seems to think. It is a matter of Hamlet's whole deportment, in which I feel we may legitimately see the deportment of a man who has been "illuminated" in the tragic sense. Bradley's term for it is fatalism, but if this is what we wish to call it, we must at least acknowledge that it is fatalism of a very distinctive kind—a kind that Shakespeare has been willing to touch with the associations of the saying in St. Matthew about the fall of a sparrow, and with Hamlet's recognition that a divinity shapes our ends. The point is not that Hamlet has suddenly become religious; he has been religious all through the play. The point is that he has now learned, and accepted, the boundaries in which human action, human judgment, are enclosed.

Till his return from the voyage he had been trying to act beyond these, had been encroaching on the role of providence, if I may exaggerate to make a vital point. He had been too quick to take the burden of the whole world and its condition upon his limited and finite self. Faced with a task of sufficient difficulty in its own right, he had dilated it into a cosmic problem—as indeed every task is, but if we think about this too precisely we cannot act at all. The whole time is out of joint, he feels, and in his young man's egocentricity, he will set it right. Hence he misjudges Ophelia, seeing in her only a breeder of sinners. Hence he misjudges himself, seeing himself a vermin crawling between earth and heaven. Hence he takes it upon himself to be his mother's conscience, though the ghost has warned that this is no fit task for him, and returns to repeat the warning: "Leave her to heaven, And to those thorns that in her bosom lodge." Even with the king, Hamlet has sought to play at God. *He* it must be who decides the issue of Claudius's salvation, saving him for a more damnable occasion. Now, he has learned that there are limits to the before and after that human reason can comprehend. Rashness, even, is sometimes good. Through rashness he has saved his life from the commission for his death, "and prais'd be rashness for it." This happy circumstance and the unexpected arrival of the pirate ship make it plain that the roles of life are not entirely self-assigned. "There is a divinity that shapes our ends, Rough-hew them how we will." Hamlet is ready now for what may happen, seeking neither to foreknow it nor avoid it. "If it be now, 'tis not to come; if it be not to come, it will be now; if it be not now, yet it will come: the readiness is all."

The crucial evidence of Hamlet's new frame of mind, as I understand it, is the graveyard scene. Here, in its ultimate symbol, he confronts, recognizes, and accepts the condition of being man. It is not simply that he now accepts death, though Shakespeare shows him accepting it in ever more poignant forms: first, in the imagined persons of the politician, the courtier, and the lawyer, who laid their little schemes "to circumvent God," as Hamlet puts it, but now lie here; then in Yorick, whom he knew and played with as a child; and then in Ophelia. This last death tears from him a final cry of passion, but the striking contrast between his behavior and Laertes's reveals how deeply he has changed.

Still, it is not the fact of death that invests this scene with its peculiar power. It is instead the haunting mystery of life itself that Hamlet's speeches point to, holding in its inscrutable folds those other mysteries that he has wrestled with so long. These he now knows for what they are, and lays them by. The mystery of evil is present here—for this is after all the universal graveyard, where, as the clown says humorously, he holds up Adam's profession; where the scheming politician, the hollow courtier, the tricky lawyer, the emperor and the clown and the beautiful young maiden, all come together in an emblem of the world; where even, Hamlet murmurs, one might expect to stumble on "Cain's jawbone, that did the first murther." The mystery of reality is here too—for death puts the question, "What is real?" in its irreducible form, and in the end uncovers all appearances: "Is this the fine of his fines and the recovery of his recoveries, to have his fine pat full of fine dirt?" "Now get you to my lady's chamber, and tell her, let her paint an inch thick, to this favor she must come." Or if we need more evidence of this mystery, there is the anger of Laertes at the lack of ceremonial trappings, and the ambiguous character of Ophelia's own death. "Is she to be buried in Christian burial when she wilfully seeks her own salvation?" asks the gravedigger. And last of all, but most pervasive of all, there is the mystery of human limitation. The grotesque nature of man's little joys, his big ambitions. The fact that the man who used to bear us on his back is now a skull that smells; that the noble dust of Alexander somewhere plugs a bung-hole; that "Imperious Caesar, dead and turn'd to clay, Might stop a hole to keep the wind away." Above all, the fact that a pit of clay is "meet" for such a guest as man, as the gravedigger tells us in his song, and yet that, despite all frailties, and limitations, "That skull had a tongue in it and could sing once."

After the graveyard and what it indicates has come to pass in him, we know that Hamlet is ready for the final contest of mighty opposites. He accepts the world as it is, the world as a duel, in which, whether we know it or not, evil holds the poisoned rapier and the poisoned chalice waits; and in which, if we win at all, it costs not less than everything. I think we understand by the close of Shakespeare's *Hamlet* why it is that unlike the other tragic heroes he is given a soldier's rites upon the stage. For as William Butler Yeats once said, "Why should we honor those who die on the field of battle? A man may show as reckless a courage in entering into the abyss of himself."

Notes

1. *Othello,* Act I, Sc. 2, 59.
2. *Ibid,* Act IV, Sc. 2, 67-69.
3. *Ibid,* Act V, Sc. 2, 3-5.
4. *Ibid,* Act V, Sc. 2, 340-48.
5. *Hamlet,* Act I, Sc. 2, 83-86.
6. *Ibid,* Act III, Sc. 1, 150-54.

*Hamlet as Minister and Scourge

When Hamlet is first preparing to leave his mother's chamber after harrowing her to repentance, he turns to the dead body of Polonius:

> For this same lord,
> I do repent; but heaven hath pleas'd it so,
> To punish me with this, and this with me,
> That I must be their scourge and minister.
> I will bestow him, and will answer well
> The death I gave him.
>
> (Act III, Sc. 4, 172-177)

These provocative, if not enigmatic, lines have received comparatively small attention. In my opinion they contain perhaps the clearest analy-

*By Fredson Bowers. From *PMLA,* LXX (1955).

sis Hamlet makes of his predicament, and are therefore worth a scrupulous enquiry.

The Variorum quotes Malone's paraphrase, "To punish me by making me the instrument of this man's death, and to punish this man by my hand." This is surely the literal meaning of the first lines. Going beyond Malone by seeking the nature of Hamlet's punishment, both Dover Wilson and Kittredge agree that "To punish me with this" means, substantially, that Hamlet perceives his secret will be revealed to Claudius, with serious consequences to himself. Kittredge writes, "the King will at once perceive that he killed Polonius by mistake for him, and will take measures accordingly." And Dover Wilson (quoting "This man shall set me packing"): "The death of Polonius has placed Hamlet within the power of the King."

This view is only superficially plausible, and it should not satisfy as offering the complete, or even the true, interpretation. The reason for Heaven's punishment is left unexamined, and no account is taken of the close syntactical relationship between the first statement about the double punishment, and the second, "That I must be their [i.e., Heaven's] scourge and minister."

For a moment let us look at this second statement. Kittredge comes near to the meaning: "heaven's scourge (of punishment) and heaven's agent—minister of divine retribution." This implies a difference between a scourge and a minister, that is, between an instrument of punishment and one of divine retribution; but how retribution differs from punishment is not indicated, nor is the question considered why Hamlet describes himself in both capacities.

In cases of doubt it is always well to work back through the text. "For this same lord, I do repent." In spite of whatever callousness Hamlet exhibits in "Thou wretched, rash, intruding fool, farewell!" and in "I'll lug the guts into the neighbour room," or in "Safely stow'd," his stated repentance must be based on more than merely practical considerations that now the hunt will be up. Although Polonius' folly has been punished by Hamlet, yet an innocent man has been killed, and Hamlet has stained his hands with blood without attaining his main objective. His attempt at revenge has led him to commit a murder which he had never contemplated. A modern audience is less likely to feel the horror of Polonius' death than an Elizabethan, which would have known from the moment the rapier flashed through the arras that Hamlet was thereafter a doomed man. On the Elizabethan stage, blood demanded blood; and at the most only two or three tragic characters who draw blood for private motives survive the denouement, and then only at the expense of a retirement to the cloister for the rest of their lives.[1]

Hamlet, no bloody madman, may well repent that he has killed an innocent person. This mistake does not excuse him. Elizabethan law, like ours, was very clear that if by premeditation one kills, but acci-

138

dentally mistakes the object and slays the wrong man, the case was still premeditated murder in the first degree, not manslaughter.[2]

Hamlet repents at the personal level, yet adds, "but heaven hath pleas'd it so,/To punish me with this." There are two implications here. First, Hamlet recognizes that his repentance cannot wash the blood from his hands, and that he must accept whatever penalty is in store for him. Second, the "this" with which he is punished is certainly the body of Polonius, and thus the fact of murder, carrying with it the inevitable penalty for blood. To view heaven's punishment as no more than the exposure of Hamlet's intents to Claudius, so that the revenge will thereafter be made more difficult, is a shallow concept which ignores the blood that has just been shed in defiance of divine law. I am concerned that the primary implication be made clear: Hamlet feels that it has pleased Heaven to punish him with the central fact of murder and one that bore no relation to his mission of justice; moreover, that he has killed the wrong man is an essential part of this punishment.

If Heaven's punishment is taken merely as the revelation of Hamlet's secret to Claudius, with all the consequences that are sure to follow, the punishment would have been comparatively mild, for the play-within-a-play had already effectively revealed Hamlet to Claudius, as well as Claudius to Hamlet. If we carefully follow the implications of the action within the setting of the time-scheme, it is clear that immediately following the mousetrap, and before the killing of Polonius, Claudius has seen Hamlet's murderous intents and has set on foot a plot to kill him. When first conceived after the eavesdropping on Hamlet and Ophelia in the nunnery scene, the English voyage was an innocent expedient to get a peculiarly behaving Hamlet out of the country, perhaps to his cure. However, it becomes a murderous scheme immediately after the play-within-a-play when Claudius changes the ceremonious details and plans to send Hamlet away in the same ship with Rosencrantz and Guildenstern, a necessary factor for the altered commission ordering Hamlet's execution in England. No hint is given that Claudius has altered the original commission in the short interval between the Queen's announcement of Polonius' death and the appearance of Hamlet before him for questioning, nor would there have been time. We learn only that Polonius' death must expedite Hamlet's departure; and hence we are required to assume that the discussion of the commission immediately following the mousetrap play involved what we later learn to have been the important change commanding Hamlet's death. Viewed in this light, the dead body of Polonius cannot punish Hamlet by revealing his secret to Claudius, for that has previously been revealed, and Claudius has already set on foot a lethal plot to dispose of his stepson.

Of course, Hamlet does not know of the change in the purport of the commission, it might be argued. But it would be most difficult to argue that Hamlet was not quite aware that in stripping the truth from Claudius by the doctored-up *Murder of Gonzago,* he had simultaneously revealed himself. The circumstances and language of the play were too damning for him to think that more than the façade of pretense could stand between him and Claudius after that episode. Hence I take it that the conventional interpretation of Hamlet's words ignores their deeper religious significance, and offers only a meaningless redundancy as a substitute.

> but heaven hath pleas'd it so,
> To punish me with this, and this with me,
> That I must be their scourge and minister.

We may paraphrase thus: Heaven has contrived this killing as a means of punishing us both and as a means of indicating to me that I must be its scourge and minister.

One need only dig down to this bare meaning to reveal how little the basic ideas have really been explained. Three difficult questions immediately assert themselves. Why was Heaven punishing Hamlet by making him the instrument of Polonius' death? Why does this punishment place him in the position of scourge and minister? What is the difference, if any, between scourge and minister? These are best answered, perhaps, in inverse order. The standard religious concept of the time was that God intervened in human affairs in two ways, internally and externally. Internally, God could punish sin by arousing the conscience of an individual to a sense of grief and remorse, which might in extraordinary cases grow so acute as to lead to madness. Externally, God worked through inanimate, or at least sub-human objects, through the forces of Nature, and through the agency of human beings. God's vengeance might strike a criminal by causing a sudden and abnormal mortal sickness, by sinking him in a squall at sea, by hitting him over the head with a falling timber, by leading him accidentally into a deep quicksand or unseen pool. The Elizabethans, if there was any suspected reason, were inclined to see God's hand in most such accidents. But sometimes Heaven punished crime by human agents, and it was standard belief that for this purpose God chose for His instruments those who were already so steeped in crime as to be past salvation. This was not only a principle of economy, but a means of freeing God from the impossible assumption that He would deliberately corrupt innocence. When a human agent was selected to be the instrument of God's vengeance, and the act of vengeance on the guilty necessitated the performance by the agent of a crime, like murder, only a man already damned for his sins was selected, and he was called a scourge.[3]

Any man who knew himself to be such a scourge knew both his function and his fate: his powers were not his own. Taking the long view, no matter how much he could glory in the triumphs of the present, his position was not an enviable one. Any human agent used by God to visit wrath and to scourge evil by evil was already condemned. This idea is clearly stated at the end of Fletcher's *Maid's Tragedy:*

> on lustful kings
> Unlook'd-for sudden deaths from God are sent;
> But curs'd is he that is their instrument.

When Hamlet called himself a scourge of Heaven, it is inconceivable that the Elizabethan audience did not know what he meant, and that Hamlet did not realize to the full what he was saying.

Although some writers, as in Fortescue's translation *The Forest,* [4] used scourge and minister interchangeably, there was a general tendency to distinguish them. The references in the concordance show, for our purposes, that Shakespeare always means minister in a good sense unless he specifies that the minister is of hell. A minister of God, in contrast to a scourge, is an agent who directly performs some good. In this sense, heavenly spirits are ministers of grace, as Hamlet calls them. The good performed by a human minister, however, may be some positive good in neutral or in good circumstances, or it may be some good which acts as a direct retribution for evil by overthrowing it and setting up a positive good in its place. The distinction between minister and scourge, thus, lies in two respects. First, a retributive minister may visit God's wrath on sin but only as the necessary final act to the overthrow of evil, whereas a scourge visits wrath alone, the delayed good to rest in another's hands. To take a rough and ready example, Richard III was thought of as a scourge for England, the final agent of God's vengeance for the deposition and murder of the anointed Richard II; but the good wishes of the ghosts make young Henry Richmond, in Raleigh's description, "the immediate instrument of God's justice," that is, a minister who will bring to a close God's wrath by exacting public justice in battle on the tyrant Richard, this triumph to be followed by a reign of peace and glory under the Tudor dynasty. In the second respect, as a contrast to the evil and damned scourge, if a minister's duty is to exact God's punishment or retribution as an act of good, his hands will not be stained with crime. If in some sense he is the cause of the criminal's death, the means provided him by Heaven will lie in some act of public justice, or of vengeance, rather than in criminal private revenge.

We are now in a position to examine Hamlet's "scourge and minister." We must recognize that the Ghost's command, though not explicit, was at first interpreted by Hamlet as a call to an act of private blood-revenge. Yet there is no getting around the fact that to an Elizabethan audience this was a criminal act of blood, not to be condoned by God, and therefore represented a particularly agonizing position for a tragic hero to be placed in. If Hamlet hopes to right the wrong done him and his father, and to ascend the throne of Denmark with honor, he must contrive a public vengeance which will demonstrate him to be a minister of Heaven's justice. Yet the secret murder of his father, so far as he can see, prevents all hope of public justice; and therefore the circumstances appear to him to enforce a criminal private revenge even after he realizes that he has been supernaturally appointed as minister. The enormous contrast between Hamlet's first promise to sweep to his revenge and his concluding, "The time is out of joint. O cursed spite,/ That ever I was born to set it right," has often been remarked, but not sufficiently against this background. Moreover, it has not been well considered that if the Ghost is a spirit of health, it could not escape from purgatory under its own volition in order to influence affairs on earth. Since divine permission alone could free the Ghost to revisit the earth, the Ghost's demand for the external punishment of Claudius, and its prophecy of the internal punishment of Gertrude, is not alone a personal call but in effect the transmission of a divine command, appointing Hamlet as God's agent to punish the specific criminal, Claudius.

With the final line of *The Maid's Tragedy* in our ears—"But curs'd is he that is their instrument"—we may see with full force the anomalous position Hamlet conceives for himself: is he to be the private-revenger scourge *or* the public-revenger minister? If scourge, he will make his own opportunities, will revenge murder with murder, and by this means visit God's wrath on corruption. If minister, God will see to it that a proper opportunity is offered in some way that will keep him clear from crime, one which will preserve him to initiate a good rule over Denmark. This crux for Hamlet has not been really pointed up, in part because Shakespeare had no need to make it explicit for his own audience.

As a consequence, Hamlet at the start finds himself in this peculiarly depressing position. He has been set aside from other human beings as an agent of God to set right the disjointed times, and he may reasonably assume from the circumstances of the ghostly visitation that he is a minister. Every private emotion urges him to a personal revenge of blood as the only means of solving his problem, and this revenge seems enforced by the secrecy of the original crime. But if he acts thus, he will be anticipating God's will, which in its good time will provide the just opportunity. If he anticipates and revenges, he risks damnation. If he does not revenge, he must torture himself with his seeming incompetence. In moments of the deepest depression, it could be natural for doubts to arise as to his role, and whether because of his "too too sullied flesh" he may not in fact have been appointed as a scourge, in which case his delay is indeed cowardly. Finally, there arises the important doubt whether the Ghost has been a demon to delude him into damning his soul by the murder of an innocent man, or indeed an agent of Heaven appointing him to an act of justice.

With these considerations in mind, the two months' delay between the Ghost's visitation and the next appearance of Hamlet in Act II may seem to have more validity than certain rather bloodthirsty critics will allow. I suggest that this delay, which Shakespeare never explicitly motivates, was caused not alone by rising doubts of the Ghost, or by the physical difficulties of getting at Claudius, or by the repugnance of a sensitive young man to commit an act of murder, or by his examining the circumstances so over-scrupulously as to become lost in the mazes of thought, motive, and doubt; but instead as much as anything by Hamlet as minister waiting on the expected opportunity which should be provided him, and not finding it.[5] The strain is, of course, tremendous, and it gives rise not only to his depressed musing on life and death in "To be or not to be" but also to the self-castigation of "O what a rogue and peasant slave." The corruption of the world, of men and women, and of Denmark with its interfering Polonius, its complaisant Ophelia, its traitorous Rosencrantz and Guildenstern whose love has been bought away from their schoolfellow—but especially of Denmark's source of corruption, its murderer-King and lustful, incestuous Queen—seem to cry out for scourging. To satisfy at least one question, he contrives the mousetrap and secures his answer, in the process revealing himself. And immediately an opportunity is given him for private revenge in the prayer scene, but one so far different from divinely appointed public vengeance that Heaven would never have provided it for its minister, a sign that the time is not yet. He passes on, racking himself with blood-thirsty promises, and—no longer trusting to Heaven's delays—impulsively takes the next action upon himself. He kills Polonius, thinking him the King. He repents, but does not expect his repentance to alter the scales of justice. Heaven, it is clear, has punished him for anticipating by his own deed the opportunity that was designed for the future. The precise form of the punishment consists in the fact that in killing, he has slain the wrong man; and the fact that it was Polonius and not the King behind the arras is the evidence for Heaven's punishment. He has irretrievably stained his hands with innocent blood by his usurping action, and foreseeing Heaven withheld his proper victim as its punishment.[6]

As I interpret it, therefore, Hamlet is not only punished *for* the murder of Polonius but *with* his murder, since Polonius was not his assigned victim; hence this fact is the evidence for Heaven's displeasure at his private revenge. The punishment *for* the murder will come, as indeed it does: it is this incident which for the Elizabethan audience motivated the justice of the tragic catastrophe and makes the closet scene the climax of the play.[7] Hamlet's words show his own recognition that he has in part made himself a scourge by the mistaken murder; and I suggest that it is his acceptance of this part of his total role that leads him to send Rosencrantz and Guildenstern so cheerfully, at least on the surface, to their doom. In his mind they are of the essence of the court's corruption under Claudius. They are adders fanged.

When next we see Hamlet, after the interlude of the graveyard scene, a manifest change has taken place. When he left for England, as shown by his "How all occasions do inform against me" soliloquy, he was still torn by his earlier dilemma of somehow reconciling the combat of his private emotions for revengeful action against the restraint of waiting on divine will. But it appears to him that very shortly Heaven reversed its course and actively demonstrated its guidance by preserving his life from the King's plot and returning him to Denmark, short-circuiting the delay of an English adventure. The conflict has certainly been resolved, and it is a different Hamlet indeed who tells Horatio that "There's a divinity that shapes our ends,/Rough-hew them how we will." He directly imputes his unsealing of the commission to heavenly prompting, and Heaven was even ordinant in providing him with his father's signet to reseal the papers. The pirates, it is clear, were only the natural culmination of Heaven's intervention on his side to bring him back to Denmark for the long-withheld vengeance.

When he recapitulates his wrongs, a new and quite different item is appended. It is true that Claudius, as he says, has killed his father, whored his mother, popped in between the election and his hopes, and has even attempted Hamlet's life by treacherous device. He demands for these, "Is't not perfect conscience/To quit him with this arm?" And then, significantly, he adds, "And is't not to be damn'd/To let this canker of our nature come/To further evil?" This is a note not heard before, an argument which would be used not by a private revenger but by one seeking public vengeance and justice. It says in effect: knowing what I know now, especially in this attempt on my life, I should be an accessory before the fact, and thus equally guilty with Claudius, if by further delay I permit him to enact more crimes. I should be directly responsible for further evil effects, and therefore I must see that his crimes are stopped.

Shakespeare here, as elsewhere, gives Hamlet no precise plan. But the note of confidence, not hitherto heard, is of the utmost importance. Before, when the ways of God were not at all apparent to his mind, we had "O what a rogue and peasant slave," or "How all occasions do inform against me." Now he says to Horatio, "The interim is mine," serene in trust that divine providence will guide him. Critics have noted this end to self-recrimination and conflict but have thought it odd that his confidence was based on no definite plan of action. Properly viewed, that is the precise point and it is one of great importance. His lack of plan and thus his insistence on providence arises from his confidence in Heaven. This is not lip-service or religious commonplace, but the very heart of the matter.

144

Immediately, Claudius' counterplot begins and the fencing match is arranged. Hamlet's assured feeling that he is only an instrument in the hands of God sustains him against the ominous portent of disaster that seizes on his heart. For he has learned his lesson from the results of killing Polonius. "There's a special providence in the fall of a sparrow," he says to Horatio; "if it be not now, yet it will come"; and, finally, the summation, "The readiness is all."

From the Elizabethan point of view, divine providence works out the catastrophe with justice. The plotters are hoist by their own villainous schemes; and then, triumphantly, the opportunity is given Hamlet to kill Claudius in circumstances which relieve him from immortal penalty for blood. By stage doctrine he must die for the slaying of Polonius, and, more doubtfully, for that of Rosencrantz and Guildenstern perhaps, the first in which he was inadvertently and the second consciously a scourge; and that penalty is being exacted. Since he cannot now ascend the throne over Claudius' body, all possible self-interest is removed. He has not plotted Claudius' death in cold blood, but seized an opportunity which under no circumstances he could have contrived by blood-revenge, to kill as a dying act of public justice a manifest and open murderer, exposed by the death of Gertrude, while himself suffering the pangs of death as his victim. The restitution of right lies only in him. Despite the terrible action of his forcing the poisoned cup between the King's teeth, Shakespeare takes great pains to remove the blood guilt from Hamlet by the expiation of his own death, and to indicate that the open killing was a ministerial act of public justice accomplished under the only possible circumstances. Hamlet's death is sufficient to expiate that of Polonius in the past and of Laertes in the present. With Christian charity Hamlet accepts Laertes' repentance and forgiveness accompanied by the prayer that "Mine and my father's death come not upon thee" in the future life; and in turn he prays that Heaven will make Laertes free from the guilt of his own. Finally, Horatio's blessing, "Flights of angels sing thee to thy rest," are words of benediction for a minister of providence who died through anticipating heavenly justice but, like Samson, was never wholly cast off for his tragic fault and in the end was honored by fulfilling divine plan in expiatory death. In more ways than one, but not necessarily more than he meant by his prophecy, Hamlet kept his promise for Polonius, "I will answer well the death I gave him."

Notes

1. As in Marston's *Antonio's Revenge* and Fletcher's *Bloody Brother*. See also my *Elizabethan Revenge Tragedy* (Princeton Univ. Press, 1940), pp. 11-12, 39-40.

2. *Elizabethan Revenge Tragedy,* p. 9.

3. Roy Battenhouse, *Marlowe's "Tamburlaine"* (Vanderbilt Univ. Press, 1941), pp. 13-15, 108-113.

4. See Battenhouse, p. 13, for a typical quotation.

5.   Strongly corroborative is the evidence of Tourneur's *Atheist's Tragedy,* a play manifestly influenced by *Hamlet* and one which carries this situation to its logical conclusion.

6.   That Heaven was behind all acts of reward or punishment is so much an article of Elizabethan tragic doctrine as to be instantly accepted at its face value by the audience without scrupulous enquiry into the hidden workings by which Heaven produced the results. Nor is it likely that Shakespeare worried much about the exact method or implications of this working in the situation in question. Heaven could readily order the ironic accident which, as a punishment, placed Polonius rather than Claudius behind the arras. However, with the proviso that there is no need to believe that Shakespeare or his audience sought out the implications in full detail, it may be remarked that the action of Heaven was theologically explicable. The crucial point is the distinction between foreknowledge and fore-ordination. It cannot be taken that Heaven fore-ordained that Hamlet should disobey and impulsively attempt revenge before Heaven had provided the opportunity and means for exhibiting the act as one of justice. On the other hand, one cannot limit the knowledge of God; and thus Heaven could foresee that Hamlet would perform this action. Conditional upon this foreknowledge, therefore, Heaven orders it so that Polonius substitutes for Claudius. The actions of Heaven conditional upon God's knowledge of the future are theologically quite different from Heaven's preordination, which wills certains events to take place.

7.   This point needs emphasis because the prayer scene is still occasionally cited as the climax. The climax is that scene in a play in which an action occurs which tips the scales for or against the fate of the protagonist in terms of the future action. The arguments for the prayer scene as the climax are superficial, for they turn only on the point that Hamlet suffers death in the catastrophe because he spared Claudius in this scene. Two considerations are always present in a tragedy. First, the climax must directly produce a train of action that leads to the catastrophe. Second, if we may briefly define tragedy as a series of morally determinate actions, the climactic scene must involve a morally determined action which justifies the tragic catastrophe to come. If we survey the prayer scene according to these two considerations, we may see that neither applies. Plotwise, no train of action results from the sparing of Claudius. Claudius' own plan, the English voyage with its deadly ending, has already been set in motion, but is to prove abortive. On the contrary, as a direct result of the killing of Polonius the plot picks up Laertes as his revenger. Claudius' own plan of the poisoned cup backfires and is one of the means for his downfall, but Laertes' plan succeeds and is the immediate cause of Hamlet's death. By a direct and continuous line of action the catastrophe goes back to the killing of Polonius. What the action of the play would have been like if Laertes had not had the occasion to revenge the death of his father, we cannot tell. This in itself is enough to remove the prayer scene from consideration as the climax from the point of view of the plot. As for the second requirement—the morally determinate action—if Hamlet's sparing of Claudius is to be a tragic error of such magnitude as to make his subsequent death an act of justice, we must take it that he should have killed Claudius at prayer. This would require the audience to be convinced that Hamlet's decision was wrong in the light of his belief that Claudius was in a state of grace. It is difficult to see how such a theory could be defended. On the other hand, if the ethical climax is to coincide with the plot climax, as it should, we are forced into examining the killing of Polonius as a morally determined action. Greek tragedy might have made of this scene a study of simple fatal error, something like Oedipus slaying his father, and drawn the moral of the ways in which fate interferes with human life. But the Elizabethan is not the Greek drama, and the English tragic writers would have agreed with Milton's God who pronounces, "What I will is Fate." The general Christian framework of Elizabethan tragic ethics demands that the slaying of Polonius be more than an unlucky accident. So far as I can see, the only way to give it a moral determinism is to argue, as I do, that it was a real error for Hamlet to attempt his private revenge at this time when Heaven had put him in a position of a minister for whom public justice would be arranged at Heaven's own pleasure. The tragic error consists in the fact that Hamlet's emotional

drive is too strong to permit him to wait upon what appears to him to be Heaven's extra-ordinary delay. Paradoxically, therefore, the tragic fact is not Hamlet's delay except for its effect upon his cumulative impatience, but instead his attempt at action. Once again, Tourneur's *Atheist's Tragedy* must be cited, with its protagonist who is in the same fix but who successfully overcomes the temptation to anticipate Heaven and who therefore survives.

Selected Criticisms

I believe the character of Hamlet may be traced to Shakespeare's deep and accurate science in mental philosophy. Indeed, that this char-acter must have some connection with the common fundamental laws of our nature may be assumed from the fact that Hamlet has been the darling of every country in which the literature of England has been fostered. In order to understand him, it is essential that we should reflect on the constitution of our own minds. Man is distinguished from the brute animals in proportion as thought prevails over sense; but in the healthy processes of the mind, a balance is constantly main-tained between the impressions from outward objects and the inward operations of the intellect; for if there be an overbalance in the contem-plative faculty, man thereby becomes the creature of mere meditation, and loses his natural power of action. Now, one of Shakespeare's modes of creating characters is to conceive any one intellectual or moral faculty in morbid excess, and then to place himself, Shake-speare, thus mutilated or diseased, under given circumstances. In Hamlet he seems to have wished to exemplify the moral necessity of a due balance between our attention to the objects of our senses and our meditation on the working of our minds—an *equilibrium* between the real and the imaginary worlds. In Hamlet this balance is disturbed; his thoughts and the images of his fancy are far more vivid than his actual perceptions, and his very perceptions, instantly passing through the *medium* of his contemplations, acquire, as they pass, a form and a colour not naturally their own. Hence we see a great, an almost enor-mous, intellectual activity, and a proportionate aversion to real action consequent upon it, with all its symptoms and accompanying qualities. This character Shakespeare places in circumstances under which it is obliged to act on the spur of the moment: Hamlet is brave and careless of death; but he vacillates from sensibility, and procrastinates from thought, and loses the power of action in the energy of resolve. Thus it is that this tragedy presents a direct contrast to that of *Macbeth*: the one proceeds with the utmost slowness, the other with a crowded and breathless rapidity.

Samuel Taylor Coleridge

The grounds of *Hamlet's* failure [as a work of art] are not immed-iately obvious. Mr. Robertson [J. M. Robertson, an American critic] is undoubtedly correct in concluding that the essential emotion of the

147

play is the feeling of a son towards a guilty mother. . . . This, however, is by no means the whole story. It is not merely the 'guilt of a mother' that cannot be handled as Shakespeare handled the suspicion of Othello, the infatuation of Antony, or the pride of Coriolanus. The subject might conceivably have expanded into a tragedy like these, intelligible, self-complete, in the sunlight. *Hamlet,* like the sonnets is full of some stuff that the writer could not drag to light, contemplate, or manipulate into art. And when we search for this feeling, we find it, as in the sonnets, very difficult to localize. You cannot point to it in the speeches; indeed, if you examine the two famous soliloquies you see the versification of Shakespeare, but a content which might be claimed by another, perhaps by the author of the *Revenge of Bussy d'Ambois,* Act V. Sc. 1. We find Shakespeare's *Hamlet* not in the action, not in any quotations that we might select, so much as in an unmistakable tone which is unmistakably not in the earlier play.

The only way of expressing emotion in the form of art is by finding an 'objective correlative'; in other words, a set of objects, a situation, a chain of events which shall be the formula of that *particular* emotion; such that when the external facts, which must terminate in sensory experience, are given, the emotion is immediately evoked. If you examine any of Shakespeare's more successful tragedies, you will find this exact equivalence; you will find that the state of mind of Lady Macbeth walking in her sleep has been communicated to you by a skilful accumulation of imagined sensory impressions; the words of Macbeth on hearing of his wife's death strike us as if, given the sequence of events, these words were automatically released by the last event in the series. The artistic 'inevitability' lies in this complete adequacy of the external to the emotion; and this is precisely what is deficient in *Hamlet.* Hamlet (the man) is dominated by an emotion which is inexpressible, because it is in *excess* of the facts as they appear. And the supposed identity of Hamlet with his author is genuine to this point: that Hamlet's bafflement at the absence of objective equivalent to his feelings is a prolongation of the bafflement of his creator in the face of his artistic problem. Hamlet is up against the difficulty that his disgust is occasioned by his mother, but that his mother is not an adequate equivalent for it; his disgust envelops and exceeds her. It is thus a feeling which he cannot understand; he cannot objectify it, and it therefore remains to poison life and obstruct action. None of the possible actions can satisfy it; and nothing that Shakespeare can do with the plot can express Hamlet for him. And it must be noticed that the very nature of the *données* [fundamental ideas] of the problem precludes objective equivalence. To have heightened the criminality of Gertrude would have been to provide the formula for a totally different emotion in Hamlet; it is just *because* her character is so negative and insignificant that she arouses in Hamlet the feeling which she is incapable of representing.

The 'madness' of Hamlet lay to Shakespeare's hand; in the earlier play a simple ruse, and to the end, we may presume, understood as a ruse by the audience. For Shakespeare it is less than madness and more than feigned. The levity of Hamlet, his repetition of phrase, his puns, are not part of a deliberate plan of dissimulation, but a form of emotional relief. In the character Hamlet it is the buffoonery of an emotion which he cannot express in art. The intense feeling, ecstatic or terrible, without an object or exceeding its object, is something which every person of sensibility has known; it is doubtless a subject of study for pathologists. It often occurs in adolescence: the ordinary person puts these feelings to sleep, or trims down his feelings to fit the business world; the artist keeps them alive by his ability to intensify the world to his emotions.

T. S. Eliot

I believe that we read Hamlet's speeches with interest chiefly because they describe so well a certain spiritual region through which most of us have passed and anyone in his circumstances might be expected to pass, rather than because of our concern to understand how and why this particular man entered it. I foresee an objection on the ground that I am thus really admitting his 'character' in the only sense that matters and that all characters whatever could be equally well talked away by the method I have adopted. But I do really find a distinction. . . . In Shakespeare himself I find Beatrice to be a character who could not be thus dissolved. We are interested not in some vision seen through her eyes, but precisely in the wonder of her being the girl she is. A comparison of the sayings we remember from her part with those we remember from Hamlet's brings out the contrast. On the one hand, 'I wonder that you will still be talking, Signior Benedick', 'There was a star danced and under that I was born', 'Kill Claudio'; on the other, 'The undiscovered country, from whose bourne no traveller returns', 'Use every man after his desert, and who should 'scape whipping?', 'The rest is silence.' Particularly noticeable is the passage where Hamlet professes to be describing his own character. 'I am myself indifferent honest, but yet I could accuse me of such things that it were better my mother had not borne me; I am very proud, revengeful, ambitious'. It is, of course, possible to devise some theory which explains these self-accusations in terms of character. But long before we have done so the real significance of the lines has taken possession of our imagination for ever. 'Such fellows as I' does not mean 'such fellows as Goethe's Hamlet, or Coleridge's Hamlet, or any Hamlet': it means *men* — creatures shapen in sin and conceived in iniquity — and the vast, empty visions of them 'crawling between earth and heaven' is what really counts and really carries the burden of the play.

It is often cast in the teeth of the great critics that each in painting *Hamlet* has drawn a portrait of himself. How if they were right? I would go a long way to meet Beatrice or Falstaff or Mr Jonathan Oldbuck or Disraeli's Lord Monmouth. I would not cross the room to meet Hamlet. It would never be necessary. He is always where I am. The method of the whole play is much nearer to Mr Eliot's own method in poetry than Mr Eliot suspects. Its true hero is man — haunted man — man with his mind on the frontier of two worlds, man unable to either quite to reject or quite to admit the supernatural, man struggling to get something done as man has struggled from the beginning, yet incapable of achievement because of his inability to understand either himself or his fellows or the real quality of the universe which has produced him. To be sure, some hints of more particular motives for Hamlet's delay are every now and then fadged up to silence our questions, just as some show of motives is offered for the Duke's temporary abdication in *Measure for Measure.* In both cases it is only scaffolding or machinery. To mistake these were *succedanea* [substitutions] for the real play and to try to work them up into a coherent psychology is the great error. I once had a whole batch of School Certificate answers on the "Nun's Priest's Tale' by boys whose form-master was apparently a breeder of poultry. Everything that Chaucer had said in describing Chauntecleer and Pertelote was treated by them simply and solely as evidence about the precise breed of these two birds. And, I must admit, the result was very interesting. They proved beyond doubt that Chauntecleer was very different from our modern specialized strains and much closer to the Old English 'barn-door fowl'. But I couldn't help feeling that they had missed something. I believe our attention to Hamlet's 'character' in the usual sense misses almost as much.

Perhaps I should rather say that it *would* miss as much if our behaviour when we are actually reading were not wiser than our criticism in cold blood. The critics, or most of them, have at any rate kept constantly before us the knowledge that in this play there is greatness and mystery. They were never entirely wrong. Their error, in my view, was to put the mystery in the wrong place—in Hamlet's motives rather than in that darkness which enwraps Hamlet and the whole tragedy and all who read or watch it. It is a mysterious play in the sense of being a play about mystery. Mr. Eliot suggests that 'more people have thought *Hamlet* a work of art because they found it interesting, than have found it interesting because it is a work of art'. When he wrote that sentence he must have been very near to what I believe to be the truth. The play is, above all else, *interesting.* But artistic failure is not in itself interesting, nor often interesting in any way: artistic success always is. To interest is the first duty of art; no other excellences will even begin to compensate for failure in this, and very serious faults will be covered by this, as by charity. The hypothesis that this play interests by being good and not by being bad has therefore the first claim on our consideration. The burden of proof rests on the other side. Is not the fascinated interest of the critics most naturally explained by supposing that this is the precise effect the play was written to produce? They may be finding the mystery in the wrong place; but the fact that they can never leave *Hamlet* alone, the continual groping, the sense, unextinguished by over a century of failures, that we have here something of inestimable importance, is surely the best evidence that the real and lasting mystery of our human situation has been greatly depicted.

C. S. Lewis

Claudius' virtues . . . are manifest. So are his faults—his original crime, his skill in the less admirable kind of policy, treachery, and intrigue. But I would point clearly that, in the movement of the play, his faults are forced on him, and he is distinguished by creative and wise action, a sense of purpose, benevolence, a faith in himself and those around him, by love of his Queen:

> . . . and for myself—
> My virtue or my plague, be it either which—
> She's so conjunctive to my life and soul,
> That, as the star moves not but in his sphere,
> I could not but by her.

(Act IV, Sc. 7, 12-16)

In short he is very human. Now these are the very qualities Hamlet lacks. Hamlet is inhuman. He has seen through humanity. And this inhuman cynicism, however justifiable in this case on the plane of causality and individual responsibility, is a deadly and venomous thing. Instinctively the creatures of earth, Laertes, Polonius, Ophelia, Rosencrantz and Guildenstern, league themselves with Claudius: they are of his kind. They sever themselves from Hamlet. Laertes sternly warns Ophelia against her intimacy with Hamlet, so does Polonius. They are in fact, all leagued against him, they are puzzled by him or fear him: he has no friend except Horatio, and Horatio, after the Ghost scenes, becomes a queer shadowy character who rarely gets beyond 'E'en so, my lord', 'My lord_____', and such-like phrases. The other persons are firmly drawn, in the round, creatures of flesh and blood. But Hamlet is not of flesh and blood, he is a spirit of penetrating intellect and cynicism and misery, without faith in himself or anyone else, murdering his love of Ophelia, on the brink of insanity, taking delight in cruelty, torturing Claudius, wringing his mother's heart, a poison in the midst of the healthy bustle of the court. He is a superman among men. And he is a superman because he has walked and held converse with death, and his consciousness works in terms of death and the negation of cynicism. He has seen the truth, not alone of Denmark, but of humanity, of the universe: and the truth is evil. Thus Hamlet is an element of evil in the state of Denmark. The poison of his mental existence spreads outwards among things of flesh and blood, like acid eating into metal. They are helpless before his very inactivity and fall one after the other, like victims of an infectious disease. They are strong with the strength of health—but the demon of Hamlet's mind is a stronger thing than they. Futilely they try to get him out of their country; anything to get rid of him, he is not safe. But he goes with a cynical smile, and is no sooner gone than he is back again in their midst, meditating in graveyards, at home with death. Not till it has slain all, is the demon that grips Hamlet satisfied. And last it slays Hamlet himself:

> The spirit that I have seen
> May be the devil . . .
>
> (Act II, Sc. 2, 573-74)

It was the devil of the knowledge of death, which possesses Hamlet and drives him from misery and pain to increasing bitterness, cynicism, murder, and madness. He has indeed bought converse with his father's spirit at the price of enduring and spreading Hell on earth. But however much we may sympathize with Ophelia, with Polonius, Rosencrantz, Guildenstern, the Queen, and Claudius, there is one reservation to be made. It is Hamlet who is right. What he says and thinks of them is true, and there is no fault in his logic. His own mother is indeed faithless, and the prettiness of Ophelia does in truth enclose a spirit as fragile and untrustworthy as her earthly beauty; Polonius is 'a foolish prating knave'; Rosencrantz and Guildenstern are time-servers and flatterers; Claudius, whose benevolence hides the guilt of murder, is, by virtue of that fact, 'a damned smiling villain'. In the same way the demon of cynicism which is in the mind of the poet and expresses itself in the figures of this play, has always this characteristic: it is right. One cannot argue with the cynic. It is unwise to offer him battle. For in the warfare of logic it will be found that he has all the guns.

G. Wilson Knight

Is it possible to conceive an experience more desolating to a man such as we have seen Hamlet to be; and is its result anything but perfectly natural? It brings bewildered horror, then loathing, then despair of human nature. His whole mind is poisoned. He can never see Ophelia in the same light again: she is a woman, and his mother is a woman: if she mentions the word 'brief' to him, the answer drops from his lips like venom, 'as woman's love.' The last words of the soliloquy, which is *wholly* concerned with this subject, are,

But break, my heart, for I must hold my tongue!

He can do nothing. He must lock in his heart, not any suspicion of his uncle that moves obscurely there, but that horror and loathing; and if his heart ever found relief, it was when those feelings, mingled with the love that never died out in him, poured themselves forth in a flood as he stood in his mother's chamber beside his father's marriage-bed.

If we still wonder, and ask why the effect of this shock should be so tremendous, let us observe that *now* the conditions have arisen under which Hamlet's highest endowments, his moral sensibility and his genius, become his enemies. A nature morally blunter would have felt even so dreadful a revelation less keenly. A slower and more limited and positive mind might not have extended so widely through its world the disgust and disbelief that have entered it. . . . But Hamlet has the imagination which, for evil as well as good, feels and sees all things in one. Thought is the element of his life, and his thought is infected. He cannot prevent himself from probing and lacerating the wound in his soul. One idea, full of peril, holds him fast, and he cries out in agony at it, but is impotent to free himself ('Must I remember?' 'Let me not think on't'). And when, with the fading of his passion, the vividness of this idea abates, it does so only to leave behind a boundless weariness and a sick longing for death.

And this is the time which his fate chooses. In this hour of uttermost weakness, this sinking of his whole being towards annihilation, there comes on him, bursting the bounds of the natural world with a shock of astonishment and terror, the revelation of his mother's adultery and his father's murder, and, with this, the demand on him, in the name of everything dearest and most sacred, to arise and act. And for a moment, though his brain reels and totters, his soul leaps up in passion to answer this demand. But it comes too late. It does but strike home the last rivet in the melancholy which holds him bound.

> The time is out of joint! O cursed spite
> That ever I was born to set it right,—

so he mutters within an hour of the moment when he vowed to give his life to the duty of revenge; and the rest of the story exhibits his vain efforts to fulfil this duty, his unconscious self-excuses and unavailing self-reproaches, and the tragic results of his delay.

'Melancholy,' I said, not dejection, nor yet insanity. That Hamlet was not far from insanity is very probable. His adoption of the pretence of madness may well have been due in part to fear of the reality; to an instinct of self-preservation, a fore-feeling that the pretence would enable him to give some utterance to the load that pressed on his heart and brain, and a fear that he would be unable altogether to repress such utterance. And if the pathologist calls his state melancholia, and even proceeds to determine its species, I see nothing to object to in that; I am grateful to him for emphasising the fact that Hamlet's melancholy was no mere common depression of spirits; and I have no doubt that many readers of the play would understand it better if they read an account of melancholia in a work on mental diseases. If we like to use the word 'disease' loosely, Hamlet's condition may truly be called diseased. No exertion of will could have dispelled it. Even if he had been able at once to do the bidding of the Ghost he would doubtless have still remained for some time under the cloud. It would be absurdly unjust to call *Hamlet* a study of melancholy, but it contains such a study.

But this melancholy is something very different from insanity, in anything like the usual meaning of that word. No doubt it might develop into insanity. The longing for death might become an irresistible impulse to self-destruction; the disorder of feeling and will might extend to sense and intellect; delusions might arise; and the man might become, as we say, incapable and irresponsible. But Hamlet's melancholy is some way from this condition. It is a totally different thing from the madness which he feigns; and he never, when alone or in company with Horatio alone, exhibits the signs of that madness. Nor is the dramatic use of this melancholy, again, open to the objections which would justly be made to the portrayal of an insanity which brought the hero to a tragic end. The man who suffers as Hamlet suffers—and thousands go about their business suffering thus in greater or less degree—is considered irresponsible neither by other people nor by himself: he is only too keenly conscious of his responsibility. He is therefore, so far, quite capable of being a tragic agent, which an insane person, at any rate according to Shakespeare's practice, is not. And finally, Hamlet's state is not one which a healthy mind is unable sufficiently to imagine. It is probably not further from average experience, nor more difficult to realise, than the great tragic passions of Othello, Antony or Macbeth.

A. C. Bradley

We are compelled then to take the position that there is some cause for Hamlet's vacillation which has not yet been fathomed. If this lies neither in his incapacity for action in general, nor in the inordinate difficulty of the particular task in question, then it must of necessity lie in the third possibility—namely, in some special feature of the task that renders it repugnant to him. This conclusion, that Hamlet at heart does not want to carry out the task, seems so obvious that it is hard to see how any open-minded reader of the play could avoid making it . . .

For some deep-seated reason, which is to him unacceptable, Hamlet is plunged into anguish at the thought of his father being replaced in his mother's affections by someone else. It is as if his devotion to his mother had made him so jealous for her affection that he had found it hard enough to share this even with his father and could not endure to share it with still another man. Against this thought, however, suggestive as it is, may be urged three objections. First, if it were in itself a full statement of the matter, Hamlet would have been aware of the jealousy, whereas we have concluded that the mental process we are seeking is hidden from him. Secondly, we see in it no evidence of the arousing of an old and forgotten memory. And, thirdly, Hamlet is being deprived by Claudius of no greater share in the Queen's affection than he had been by his own father, for the two brothers made exactly similar claims in this respect—namely, those of a loved husband. The last-named objection, however, leads us to the heart of the situation. How if, in fact, Hamlet had in years gone by, as a child, bitterly resented having had to share his mother's affection even with his own father, had regarded him as a rival, and had secretly wished him out of the way so that he might enjoy undisputed and undisturbed the monopoly of that affection. If such thoughts had been present in his mind in childhood days they evidently would have been 'repressed', and all traces of them obliterated, by filial piety and other educative influences. The actual realization of his early wish in the death of his father at the hands of a jealous rival would then have stimulated into activity these 'repressed' memories, which would have produced, in the form of depression and other suffering, an obscure aftermath of his childhood's conflict. This is at all events the mechanism that is actually found in the real Hamlets who are investigated psychologically.

The explanation, therefore, of the delay and self-frustration exhibited in the endeavour to fulfil his father's demand for vengeance is that to Hamlet the thought of incest and parricide combined is too intolerable to be borne. One part of him tries to carry out the task, the other flinches inexorably from the thought of it. How fain would he blot it out in that 'bestial oblivion' which unfortunately for him his conscience condemns. He is torn and tortured in an insoluble inner conflict . . .

Ernest Jones

Bibliography

Alexander, Peter. *Hamlet: Father and Son.* Oxford: The Clarendon Press, 1955.

Bowers, Fredson. *Elizabethan Revenge Tragedy.* Princeton: Princeton University Press, 1940.

Bradley, A. C. *Shakespearean Tragedy.* 2nd edition. New York: St. Martin's Press, 1978.

Campbell, Lily B. *Shakespeare's Tragic Heroes: Slaves of Passion.* New York: Cambridge University Press, 1930.

Charney, M. *Style in Hamlet.* Princeton: Princeton University Press, 1969.

Coleridge, S. T. *Coleridge's Writings on Shakespeare,* ed. T. Hawkes. New York: G. P. Putnam's Sons, 1959.

Eliot, T. S. "Hamlet and His Problems," in *Selected Essays.* New York: Harcourt, Brace and World, 1950.

Fergusson, Francis. *The Idea of a Theatre.* Princeton: Princeton University Press, 1949.

Fisch, Harold. *Hamlet and the World.* New York: Ungar, 1971.

Granville-Barker, Harley. *Prefaces to Shakespeare.* 2 vols. Princeton: Princeton University Press, 1946-47.

Grebanier, B. *The Heart of Hamlet.* New York: Thomas Y. Crowell, 1960.

Harbage, Alfred. *Shakespeare: A Reader's Guide.* New York: Farrar, Straus and Co., 1963.

Jones, Ernest. *Hamlet and Oedipus.* New York: W. W. Norton, 1949.

Knight, G. W. *The Wheel of Fire.* Rev. ed. London: Metheun, 1949.

Knights, L. C. *An Approach to Hamlet.* London: Chatto and Windus, 1960.

Levin, Harry. *The Question of Hamlet.* Oxford: Oxford University Press, 1959.

Madariaga, Salvador de. *On Hamlet.* London: Hollis and Carter, 1948.

Ribner, Irving. *Patterns in Shakespearean Tragedy.* London: Methuen, 1960.

Rosen, William. *Shakespeare and the Craft of Tragedy.* Cambridge: Harvard University Press, 1960.

Sanders, Leonard. *The Hamlet Warning.* New York: Scribner, 1976.

Schücking, L. L. *Character Problems in Shakespeare's Plays.* New York: H. Holt, 1922.

Tillyard, E. M. W. *Shakespeare's Problem Plays.* London: Chatto and Windus, 1951.

Traversi, Derek. *An Approach to Shakespeare.* New York: Doubleday, 1956.

Walker, Roy. *The Time Is Out of Joint.* London: A. Dakers, 1948.

Wilson, J. Dover. *What Happens in Hamlet.* New York: Macmillan, 1940.